# Hiking
# the Columbia
# River Gorge

**Russ Schneider**

FALCON®
HELENA, MONTANA

**A FALCON GUIDE** ®

Falcon® is continually expanding its list of recreational guidebooks. All books include detailed descriptions, accurate maps, and all the information necessary for enjoyable trips. You can order extra copies of this book and get information and prices for other Falcon® guidebooks by writing Falcon, P.O. Box 1718, Helena, MT 59624 or calling toll-free 1-800-582-2665. Also, please ask for a free copy of our current catalog. Visit our website at http:\\www.falconguide.com.

©1997 by Falcon® Publishing, Inc., Helena, Montana.
Printed in the United States of America.

3 4 5 6 7 8 9 0 MG 03 02 01 00 99 98

Falcon and FalconGuide are registered trademarks of Falcon® Publishing, Inc.

Cover photo by Peter Marbach/Borland Stock.
All black-and-white photos by Russ Schneider.

Library of Congress Cataloging-in-Publication Data

Schneider, Russ.
    Hiking the Columbia River Gorge / by Russ Schneider.
       p.   cm.
    ISBN 1-56044-568-8
    1.  Hiking--Columbia River Gorge (Or. and Wash.)--Guidebooks.
  2.   Columbia River Gorge (Or. and Wash.)--Guidebooks.   I.  Title.
GV199.42.C58S34    1997
917.9704'43--dc21                                97-17528
                                                    CIP

CAUTION
Outdoor recreational activities are by their very nature potentially hazardous. All participants in such activities must assume the responsibility for their own actions and safety. The information contained in this guidebook cannot replace sound judgment and good decision-making skills, which help reduce risk exposure, nor does the scope of this book allow for disclosure of all the potential hazards and risks involved in such activities.

    Learn as much as possible about the outdoor recreational activities in which you participate, prepare for the unexpected, and be cautious. The reward will be a safer and more enjoyable experience.

 Text pages printed on recycled paper.

*The Columbia River Highway has not only unlocked the way to the very heart of the wonder region but it has thrown wide the door, and all are bidden to enter and to enjoy the thrill of intimate touch with one of nature's most stupendous bits of handiwork.*

—Ira Williams 1916

# CONTENTS

# CONTENTS

# ACKNOWLEDGMENTS

Special thanks to Karen, Peter, Nghia, and Susan for hiking with me.

I would not have completed this book without the help of many knowledgeable commentators. I would like to thank Charlie Quin of the Nature Conservancy, Mike Ferris of the Columbia River Gorge National Scenic Area, Claudia at the Skamania Lodge Forest Service Visitor Center, Ron and Katie Goodwin of the Friends of Multnomah Falls, Steve Johnson at Washington State Parks, Peter Martin at Mount Hood Ranger District, and Randall Green at Falcon.

I also believe that anyone who hikes in the Gorge should thank Duffy Dufresne and his USFS trail crew for the incredible job they do of managing almost 200 miles of trails under heavy use and adverse weather conditions like ice floods and mudslides. Think about that the next time there are a lot of slides in the Gorge. Those trails won't stay uncleared for long.

And most importantly, love and hugs to my wife, Kimberly.

# MAP LEGEND

| | | | |
|---|---|---|---|
| Interstate | | Campground, Picnic Area | |
| US Highway | | Cabins/Buildings | |
| State or Other Principal Road | | Peak | 9,782 ft. |
| National Park Route | | Hill | |
| Forest Road | 000 | Elevation | 9,782 ft. |
| Interstate Highway, Exit | | Gate | |
| Paved Road | | Mine Site | |
| Gravel Road | | Overlook/Point of Interest | |
| Unimproved Road | | Bridge, Tunnel | |
| Trailhead | | National Forest/Park Boundary | |
| Main Trail(s) /Route(s) | | Lake | |
| Alternate/Secondary Trail(s)/Route(s) | | Map Orientation | N |
| Parking Area | P | Scale | 0   0.5   1  Miles |
| River/Creek, Waterfall | | Cliff | Top Edge |
| Intermittent Stream | | | |
| Spring | | | |

# USGS TOPOGRAPHIC MAP INDEX

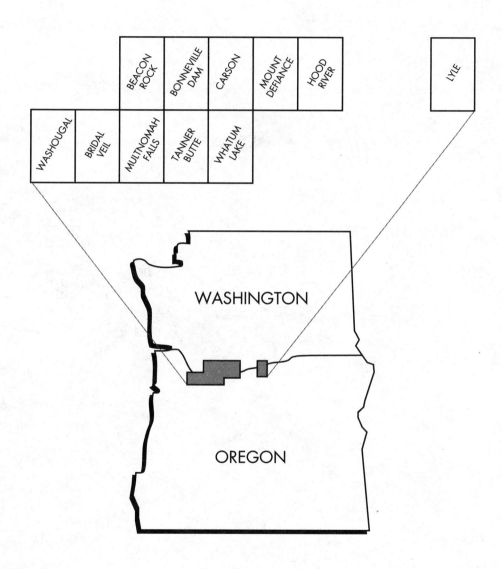

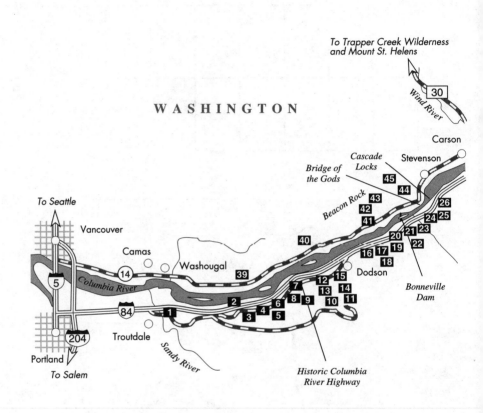

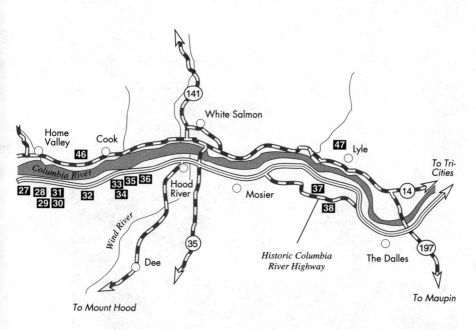

141

White Salmon

Home
Valley

Cook

47 Lyle

46

*Columbia River*

To Tri-
Cities

33 35 36

27 28 31

32

34

Hood
River

29 30

Mosier

37

38

14

*Wind River*

35

Historic Columbia
River Highway

The Dalles

197

Dee

To Maupin

To Mount Hood

N

0    3    6

Miles

O R E G O N

WASHINGTON

OREGON

*Misty Multnomah Falls*

# INTRODUCTION

**The Great Passage to the Pacific**

One of the things that makes Washington and Oregon one of the most liveable areas in the world is the easy access to outdoor recreation. The Columbia River Gorge is one of the most beautiful areas enjoyed by residents of the Pacific Northwest. The Gorge's proximity to the metropolitan Portland and Vancouver areas and the easy access from Interstate 84 make the Columbia River Gorge a popular hiking area.

Driving through the Columbia River Gorge for the first time would fill anyone with wonder. The massive basalt cliffs and crashing waterfalls emphasize the steep walls of the Gorge. The interstate is insignificant compared to the powerful forces that carved this river's passage. A massive flood caused by the overflowing of ancient Lake Missoula originally scored out this break in the mighty Cascade Mountain Range. We can only imagine what it felt like for Lewis and Clark to reach this final passage to the Pacific. Here in the Gorge is where they first saw the rise and fall of the tides that signalled the end of their journey. Today, they might have more trouble coping with the locks than with the great rapids of the past.

The views of Mount Hood, Mount Adams, and Mount St. Helens are stunning from many Gorge trails. The Columbia River Gorge includes: Mount Hood and Gifford Pinchot National Forests, the Mark O. Hatfield Wilderness Area (formerly the Columbia Wilderness Area), the Historic Columbia River Highway, and 22 state parks. The area contains 300,000 acres of publicly accessible recreation land and over 40 trails less than two hours drive from the city. Eighty percent of the Columbia River Gorge National Scenic Area is privately owned, but is managed cooperatively by the scenic area office. There are 167 miles of maintained trails and various un-maintained and primitive routes.

In putting together this guide, I focused on trails with public access. I tried to include every hikeable trail between the Dalles and the Portland/Vancouver area. They range from 15 minute walks to 20–mile days. There are hikes for all ages and abilities. Check out the vacation planner and be on your merry way.

# A BRIEF GEOLOGIC HISTORY OF THE COLUMBIA RIVER GORGE

The geologic history of the Columbia River Gorge emphasizes three catastrophic series of events. First, a series of volcanic eruptions laid down the basalt rock and soil; next the flood of ancient Lake Missoula carved out the U-shaped valley. Finally, landslides blocked the river channel, diverting the river and forming the great cascades.

Volcanoes erupted in the Western Cascades 18 to 30 million years ago, creating a layer of volcanic ash, lava, and mud flows several miles thick. The cliffs of the Gorge expose about 1,000 feet of the mud flows.

The first in the series of catastrophic events, between 12 and 17 million years ago, were the eruptions from dozens of mile–long fissures in eastern Washington and Oregon. The flows of hot and fluid basaltic lava spread over 60,000 square miles in both states. Only 16 of the over 200 known basalt flows occurred in gorge cliffs. When a former valley of the Columbia filled with basaltic lava, the river was rerouted north, and cut a new valley. Gray andesitic lava from the volcanoes built up the surface of the Cascade plateau. The lava flows caused a final diversion of the Columbia between 2

*The Columbia River Gorge, from Angels Rest, with Hamilton and Table mountains in the distance.*

and 3 million years ago, by filling a deep canyon that it had run through. This channel is now known as the Sandy River drainage. Now in its present track, the Columbia River cut itself a deep, V-shaped canyon. The erection of the 14 major High Cascade volcanoes and more than 1,000 smaller peaks and cinder cones followed only in the last 700,000 years.

The second series of catastrophes began 15,000 years ago, near the end of the Ice Age. A glacial lobe from Canada formed an ice dam, 2,500 feet high, at Lake Pend Oreille. The dam backed water up the Clark Fork valley of Idaho and impounded Lake Missoula, an ancient lake in Montana containing one fifth of the amount of water in Like Michigan. When the lake rose high enough to wash away the dam, 500 cubic miles of water poured across eastern Washington, scouring out Grand Coulee and hundreds of miles of other coulee valleys (now high and dry). This process was repeated anywhere from 40 to 100 times or more over a 3,000 year period: the ice dams reformed, the lake refilled, and catastrophic floods reoccurred. In the Columbia River Gorge, these floods scoured away the valley walls, changed the V-shape to its present U-shape, and formed the cliffs and waterfalls along the south side of the valley. Floodwaters were 1,000 feet deep at The Dalles, topped Crown Point at 700 feet, and covered the Portland area at 400 feet.

The final geologic catastrophe was the cascade landslide upon which Bonneville now rests. Probably, a great earthquake started the landslide 750

*Mount Hood from the Pacific Crest Trail.*

years ago. Then, the flood-steeped faces of Table Mountain displaced the river more than a mile to the south, and built a debris dam 270 feet high across the river. By comparison, the modern–day Bonneville Dam is only 80 feet high. Forests along the river as far east as the Dalles were drowned as the lake filled behind the landslide debris dam. For as long as the dam existed, local Indians were able to cross the river dry shod. Eventually the dam washed away, leaving the series of Cascades of the Columbia River that we know today. But Indian memories of the dam survive in the form of the legendary "Bridge of the Gods."

—information provided by the U.S. Army Corps of Engineers

# USING THIS GUIDEBOOK

This guidebook won't answer every question you have as you plan your excursions into the Columbia River Gorge. But then, you probably don't want to know everything before you go—that would remove the thrill of making your own discoveries while exploring this magnificent landscape. However, this book will provide you with all of the basic information you need to plan a safe and exciting trip.

## ALL TRAILS START IN THE GORGE

This guide is limited in the area it covers to hikes that begin in the Columbia River Gorge, most of which are quite near the shore. Rather than cover a large area superficially, this guide covers the trails between Portland and the Dalles thoroughly.

This sometimes makes for more climbing than might otherwise be necessary. Don't feel that you have to limit yourself to following the exact routes described—feel free to hike downhill all day if you like. My knees just happen to prefer going uphill, and you get a better workout climbing. However, these hikes are equally memorable whether you go uphill or down.

## TRAFFIC

Each hike description gives the volume of traffic a rating of Light, Moderate, or Heavy. Heavy use indicates you will likely see many other hikers on a sunny day. Moderate use indicates that you probably will see other hikers, but not that many. Light use is a rating I reserve for little–used or hard–to-get-to places in the Gorge.

## DISTANCES

It's almost impossible to figure completely accurate lengths for hiking trails. The distances used in this guidebook are derived from a combination of actual experience hiking the trails, distances stated on Forest Service signs, and estimates made from looking at topo maps. In some cases, calculated distances may be slightly off, so consider this in your planning. Keep in mind that distance is often less important than difficulty—a rough and rocky cross-country trek of only 2 miles can take longer than 5 or 6 miles on a good trail.

## TRAIL DIFFICULTY RATINGS

The estimates of difficulty are subjective and serve as a general guide only, not the final word. What is difficult to one person may seem easy to the next. In this guidebook, difficulty ratings consider both how long and how strenuous the route is. Here are general definitions of the ratings:

**Easy**—Suitable for any hiker, including small children or the elderly, without serious elevation gain, off-trail or hazardous sections, or places where the trail is faint and hard to follow.

**Moderate**—Suitable for hikers who have some experience and at least an average fitness level; probably not suitable for small children or the elderly unless they have an above-average level of fitness. These trails may have some short sections where the trail is difficult to follow, and often have some big hills to climb.

**Difficult**—Suitable for experienced hikers at an above-average fitness level. Often some sections of these trails are difficult to follow or there are off-trail sections that could require knowledge of route-finding with topo map and compass. In addition these trails often involve serious elevation gain, as well as the possibility of hazardous conditions and obstacles like difficult stream crossings, snow fields, or cliffs.

**Note:** When the difficulty of a trail deserves special attention, this will be mentioned within the hike description. Some trails, like the Mount Defiance trail, are considered extreme climbs suitable only for the experienced and very fit. Please consider your fitness level before attempting any of the trails listed as Difficult Power Hikes in the Vacation Planner.

## FOLLOWING FAINT TRAILS

If a trail is described as an un-maintained route, orienteering skills are necessary, but most of these trails were at least maintained in the past and are still followable. The few Columbia Gorge trails that receive infrequent use tend to fade away in overgrown vine maple and deadfall, on ridges, or through rocky sections. Don't panic. Usually, these sections are short, and you can look ahead to see where the trail goes. Often, you can see the trail going up a hill or through a corridor of trees ahead. If so, focus on that landmark and don't worry about being off the trail for a short distance.

Watch for other indicators that you are indeed on the right route, especially when the trail isn't clearly visible. Watch for cairns, blazes, downfall cut with saws, and trees with the branches whacked off one side. Only follow official Forest Service blazes which are shaped like an "i" or upside-down exclamation point, and don't follow blazes made by hunters, outfitters, or other hikers marking the way to some special spot. Don't count on blazes. Not all trails are presently blazed.

## FINDING MAPS

Good maps are easy to find, and they are essential to any wilderness trip. For safety reasons, you need maps for route-finding and for "staying found." For non-safety reasons, you would not want to miss out on the joy of mindlessly whittling away untold hours staring at a topo map, and wondering what it's like here and there.

For trips into the Columbia River Gorge, you have several good choices for maps:

1. U.S. Geological Survey (USGS) topographic maps. Check sporting goods stores in the area or write directly to the USGS at the following address:

> Map Distribution
> U.S. Geological Survey
> Box 25286, Federal Center
> Denver, CO 80225

To make sure you order the correct USGS map, refer to the grid on page vii.

2. There is an excellent Columbia Gorge recreation map originally published by the Forest Service, called Trails of the Columbia Gorge. However, it does not include most of the trips on the Washington Side. It is available through most local USFS offices and Northwest Interpretive Asssociation outlets. It also is available from:

> Nature of the Northwest
> 800 NE Oregon Street, Suite 177
> Portland, OR 97232
> 503-872-2750

3. A series of three hiking maps published by Green Trails. You can find Green Trails maps at sporting goods stores in the area or you can write to:

> Green Trails
> P.O. Box 1272
> Bellevue, WA 98009

In addition, there are several other maps of the Columbia River Gorge which are good for a bigger picture of the entire area, and Forest Service maps of the Gifford Pinchot and Mount Hood national forests have the latest road information. A national scenic area map is now available from the Forest Service's scenic area office in Hood River. The Oregon and Washington *Atlas & Gazetteer* are good sources of map information for the northwest. All of these maps are nice to have, but not necessary. All you really need is one of the three maps listed above describing the area you plan to visit.

For Forest Service information you can call, visit, or write to the Columbia River Gorge National Scenic Area office. Or stop by the visitor center at Multnomah Falls, Skamania Lodge, or the Gorge Discovery Center:

Columbia River Gorge National Scenic Area
USDA Forest Service
902 Wasco Avenue, Suite 200
Hood River, OR 97031
541-386-2333

Multnomah Falls Forest Service Interpretive Center
503-695-2372

Skamania Lodge Forest Service Information Center
509-427-2528

Columbia Gorge Discovery Center (the Dalles)
541-296-8600

The best way to get up–to–date information on the Gorge is to call 541-386-2333 before you go. If you call the National Forest Office, this is the number they will most likely refer you to. This information is updated weekly.

For wilderness specific questions regarding the newly renamed Mark O. Hatfield Wilderness Area (Columbia Wilderness Area) call or write:

Hood River Ranger District
6780 Highway 35
Hood River-Parkdale, OR 97041
541-352-6002

---

### *SPECIAL REGULATIONS*

### Scenic Area Regulations
1. Dogs are permitted on a 6–foot leash.
2. Mountain bikes are not permitted on any Gorge trails except for Larch Mountain Loop and sections of Gorge Trail 400.
3. Horses are permitted on the Herman Creek Trail and the Pacific Crest Trail, but prohibited on all other trails.

4. Trail running is prohibited on most trails in the Gorge.
5. Some areas like Multnomah Falls have trail-specific regulations, which are listed at the beginning of each hike.
6. Motor vehicles are prohibited on trails in the Gorge.
7. Respect private property—not all open or forested lands are publicly owned.

### Mark O. Hatfield (formerly Columbia) Wilderness Regulations
1. A voluntary permit (it's free and not legally required) can be obtained at the entrance point to the wilderness area. The data from these permits, especially 1993-1995, may determine future regulation of use.
2. No campfires in the Eagle Creek Corridor, within 0.5 mile of the Eagle Creek Trail 440 to the junction with Eagle-Tanner Trail 433.
3. No campfires outside of designated sites or within 200 feet of Whatum Lake.
4. No camping outside of designated sites or within 200 feet of Whatum Lake.
5. A $3 per day or $25 per season permit is required for parking at the following trailheads in the Columbia Gorge scenic area and Mount Hood National Forest:

| Oregon | Washington |
|---|---|
| Bridge of the Gods | Bonneville |
| Eagle Creek | Catherine Creek |
| Herman Creek | Dog Mountain |
| Larch Mountain | Sams Walker |
| Wahclella | |
| Wyeth | |
| Rainy Lake | |
| Wahtum Lake | |
| Warren Lake | |

# VACATION PLANNER

### Really Easy Day Hikes
Bridal Veil Falls and Overlook Loop Trail
Falls at Shepperds Dell
Sherrard Point
Beacon Rock Nature Trail
Saint Cloud Nature Trail
Sams Walker Nature Trail
Multnomah Falls Lower Barrier Free Trail (closed by 1997 ice storm, will reopen soon)

## Easy But Not Too Easy

Latourell Falls
Horsetail and Ponytail Falls
Perham Creek Loop
Rodney and Hardy Falls
Wahclella Falls
Elowah Falls
Rowena Plateau
Coopey Falls
Rooster Rock Nature Trail

## Moderate Hikes

Multnomah Falls
Beacon Rock
Tom McCall Point
Angels Rest
Larch Mountain Loop
Wyeth Trail
Tanner Creek Trail (easy after you reach the actual trail, but the hike up the road lengthens it a bit.)
Wauna Viewpoint

## Difficult Hikes

Casey Creek Loop
Indian Point Trail
Dog Mountain Loop
Hamilton Mountain
Wygant Trail
Oneonta Trail to Larch Mountain
Larch Mountain Trail

## Difficult Power Hikes and Climber Training Hikes

Starvation Ridge
Mount Defiance
Table Mountain
Nesmith Point

## Backpacking Trips

Mount Defiance—Warren Lake
Wyeth Trail to North Lake (can be combined with trip to Warren Lake and Bear Lake)
Eagle Creek (Tanner Butte Loop option)
Oneonta Trail to Larch Mountain
Herman Creek to Whatum Lake (Pacific Crest Trail Loop option)
Gorton Creek Trail to Rainy Lake (can be combined with Wyeth or Herman Creek Trails)
Pacific Crest Trail to Whatum Lake

**If You're Not Scared of Heights (trips with steep drop-offs near the trail)**

Upper McCord Creek Falls
Beacon Rock
Rock of Ages Ridge
Munra Point
Hamilton Mountain (southern face route)
Eagle Creek
Ruckel Ridge Loop
Indian Point Loop (just the lookout)

**Waterfall Lovers' Hikes**

Latourell Falls
Bridal Veil Falls
Falls at Shepperds Dell
Coopey Falls
Wakeena Falls
Multnomah Falls
Horsetail and Ponytail Falls
Oneonta Trail to Larch Mountain
Wahclella Falls
Elowah Falls
Upper McCord Creek Falls
Eagle Creek Trail
Rodney and Hardy Falls
Pacific Crest Trail to Dry Creek Falls
Lancaster Falls

**Author's Choice**

Table Mountain
Nesmith Point
Eagle Tanner Loop
Multnomah Falls

# LEAVE NO TRACE

Nowadays, most wilderness users want to walk softly, but some aren't aware that they have poor manners. Often, their actions come from the outdated understanding of a past generation of campers who cut green boughs for evening shelters and beds, built fire rings, and dug trenches around tents. Today, such behavior is unacceptable. The wilderness is shrinking, while the number of users keeps growing. More and more camping areas show unsightly signs of this trend.

Thus, a new code of ethics is growing out of the need to cope with the unending waves of people wanting a perfect wilderness experience. Today, we all must leave no clues that we have gone before. Canoeists can look behind them and see no trace of their passing. The same should be true of wild country recreation. Enjoy the wilderness, but leave only memories behind.

1. **Most of us know better than to litter**—in or out of the wilderness. Be sure you leave nothing, regardless of how small it is, along the trail or at the campsite. This means you should pack out everything, including orange peels, flip tops, cigarette butts, and gum wrappers. Also, pick up any trash that others have left behind.

2. **Follow the main trail.** Avoid cutting switchbacks and walking on vegetation beside the trail. In the Gorge, some of the terrain is very fragile, so when going off-trail to get to a favorite lake or mountain top, do your part not to create a new trail. Leave all rocks, antlers, or wildflowers. The next person wants to see them, too. Also, safety is a concern on many of the steep off–trail slopes and cliffs. If people continue to cut switchbacks the trail crew will have to build unsightly fences along biologically sensitive areas, much like the lower part of the Multnomah Falls Trail.

3. **Avoid marking your route.** Traditionally, backcountry trails are marked by cairns or blazes. Cairns (small stacks of rocks) commonly mark confusing places on maintained trails, but avoid building cairns when traveling cross-country. They detract from the wilderness experience and can promote the repeated use of a specific route, eventually creating a new trail. Blazes, usually an upside-down exclamation point carved into the bark of trees, also mark many maintained trails, but individuals should never blaze trees in the back country.

4. **Try to camp below timberline.** Alpine areas are delicate and require special care. Often, it's only a short hike to a good campsite below timberline. When reasonable, keep your camp away from a shoreline or stream bank, setting up the tent at least 100 feet from a lake or stream. If there is already an established campsite, use it, rather than creating additional damage by establishing a new one. When fetching water, use established paths or vary your route if there are none.

5. **Campfires** probably cause more damage to the back country than any other aspect of camping. It is always better to use a lightweight camp stove instead. Although campfires are legal in most parts of the Gorge, avoid building fires in alpine areas where the surface is fragile and wood is scarce.
If a campfire is appropriate for the campsite, use the existing fire ring. If the area does not have a fire ring, don't build one. Dig out the native vegetation and topsoil and set it aside. When breaking camp douse the fire thoroughly. After it is completely out, scatter the ashes and replace the native soil and vegetation. Build fires away from trees to prevent damage to root systems. Keep fires small and widely disperse any partially burned wood.

Gather dead and down branches to burn, and avoid using a saw or ax.

Note that no campfires are permitted in the Eagle Creek Corridor.

6. **Avoid making loud noises** that may disturb others. Remember, sound travels easily to the other side of the Gorge.

7. **Be careful with food wastes** to prevent unsightly messes and bad odors. Burn all flammable food packaging if you have a fire and clean the remains out of the ashes. Always pack out garbage. Likewise, completely burn fish viscera. If fires are not allowed, place fish viscera and leftover food in plastic bags and carry it out. Never throw fish viscera into mountain streams and lakes. Broadcast waste water 100 feet from open water and trails, after sifting out chunks with a wire screen. Never wash dishes in a mountain stream or lake. If you use soap, make sure it's biodegradable.

8. **Be careful with human wastes.** Use white, unscented paper and bury it 6-8 inches deep along with human waste. Thoroughly bury human wastes to avoid any chance of bad odor or water pollution. This is a good reason to carry a lightweight trowel. Keep wastes at least 200 feet away from lakes and streams.

9. **Pack-in, pack-out.** If you carry something into the backcountry, consume it, burn it, or carry it out.

For more information on low impact camping techniques, read the books *Leave No Trace* (Falcon 1997) or *Wild Country Companion* (Falcon 1994).

# SAFETY: BE PREPARED

The Boy Scouts of America, for decades, adhered to what is perhaps the best single piece of safety advice—Be Prepared! For starters, carry survival and first-aid materials, proper clothing, a compass, and topographic maps—and know how to use them.

Perhaps the second-best advice is to tell somebody where you're going and when you plan to return. Pilots must file flight plans before every trip, and anybody venturing into a blank spot on the map should do the same. File your "flight plan" with a friend or relative before taking off.

Next to preparedness and proper equipment is physical conditioning. Being fit not only makes wilderness travel more fun, it makes it safer.

To whet your appetite for more knowledge of wilderness safety and preparedness, here are a few basic tips:

Check the weather forecast. Be careful not to get caught at high altitude by a snowstorm, and watch cloud formations closely, so you don't get stranded on a ridge line during a lightning storm. Avoid traveling during prolonged periods of cold weather.

If you start a fire, you are responsible for keeping your fire under control at all times and are accountable for the huge expense of fighting the fire and for any damage resulting from carelessness. Be extra careful if the fire danger is high. Check with the nearest Forest Service office for more information on fire danger and restrictions. If there is a fire in an area, consider that area off limits to outdoor recreation.

- Avoid traveling alone in the wilderness.
- Never split up in the backcountry.
- Withstand the temptation to swim across a high mountain lake or large stream.
- Be wary of steep snow banks with rocks or cliffs at the bottom.
- Know the preventive measures, symptoms and treatment of hypothermia, the silent killer.
- Study basic survival and first aid before leaving home.
- Don't eat wild mushrooms or other plants unless you are positive of their identification.
- Before you leave, find out as much as you can about the route, especially the potential hazards.
- Don't exhaust yourself or weaker members of your party by traveling too far or too fast. Let the slowest person set the pace.
- Don't wait until you're confused to look at your maps. Follow them as you go along, from the moment you start moving up the trail, so you have a continual fix on your location.
- If you get lost, don't panic. Sit down and relax for a few minutes while you carefully check out your topo map and take a reading with your compass. Confidently plan your next move. It's often smart to retrace your steps until you find familiar ground, even if it you think it might make the trip longer. Lots of people get temporarily lost in the wilderness and survive—usually by calmly and rationally dealing with the situation.
- Be extra cautious when fording a large stream. Use sandals or remove your socks and put your boots back on. This makes for more secure footing on the slippery stream bottom. Avoid the current's full force by keeping sideways to the flow. Slide—don't lift—your feet one at a time, making sure that one foot is securely anchored before seeking a new hold with the other one. Most often small rocks provide more stable footing than large, potentially slick rocks. Go slowly and deliberately. If you use a walking stick, keep it on the upstream side for additional support.
- Stay clear of all wild animals.
- Last but not least, don't forget that the best defense against unexpected hazards is knowledge. Read up on the latest in wilderness safety information, before you go.

## SURVIVAL KIT

A survival kit should include: compass, whistle, matches in a waterproof container, cigarette lighter, candle, emergency fishing gear (60 feet of 6-pound line, 6 hooks, 6 lead shot, and 6 trout flies), signal mirror, fire starter, aluminum foil, water purification tablets, space blanket, and flare.

## FIRST-AID KIT

Your first-aid kit should include: sewing needle, a snake-bite kit, aspirin, antibacterial ointment, 2 antiseptic swabs, 2 butterfly bandages, adhesive tape, 4 adhesive strips, 4 gauze pads, 2 triangular bandages, codeine tablets, 2 inflatable splints, moleskin, 1 roll of 3–inch gauze, CPR shield, rubber gloves, and lightweight first-aid instructions.

## HYPOTHERMIA

Be aware of the danger of hypothermia—a condition in which the body's internal temperature drops below normal. It can lead to mental and physical collapse and death.

Hypothermia results from exposure to cold and is aggravated by wetness, wind, and exhaustion. The moment you begin to lose heat faster than your body produces it, you're suffering from exposure. Your body starts involuntary exercise such as shivering to stay warm, and your body makes involuntary adjustments to preserve normal temperature in vital organs, restricting

*The Mark O. Hatfield Wilderness before the thaw.*

blood flow in the extremities. Both responses drain your energy reserves. The only way to stop the drain is to reduce the degree of exposure.

With full-blown hypothermia, your energy reserves are empty, and cold reaches the brain, depriving you of good judgment and reasoning power. You won't be aware that this is happening. You lose control of your hands. Your internal temperature slides downward. Without treatment, this slide leads to stupor, collapse, and death.

To defend against hypothermia, stay dry. When clothes get wet, they lose about 90 percent of their insulating value. Wool loses relatively less heat; cotton, down, and some synthetics lose more. Choose rain clothes that cover the head, neck, body, and legs, and provide good protection against wind-driven rain. Most hypothermia cases develop in air temperatures between 30 and 50 degrees Fahrenheit, but hypothermia can develop in warmer temperatures.

If your party travels in wind, cold, and wet, think hypothermia. Watch yourself and others for these symptoms: Uncontrollable fits of shivering; vague, slow, slurred speech; memory lapses; incoherence; immobile, fumbling hands; frequent stumbling or a lurching gait; drowsiness (to sleep is to die); apparent exhaustion; and inability to get up after a rest.

When a member of your party has hypothermia, they may deny any problem. Believe the symptoms, not the victim. Even mild symptoms demand treatment, as follows:

- Get the victim out of the wind and rain.
- Strip off all wet clothes.

If the victim has mild symptoms, give him or her warm drinks. Then, get them in warm clothes and a warm sleeping bag. Place well-wrapped water bottles filled with heated water close to the victim.

If the victim has serious symptoms, attempt to keep them awake. Put the victim in a sleeping bag with another person—both naked. If you have a double bag, put two warm people in with the victim.

---

### WOOD TICKS

Ticks are common throughout wooded, brushy, and grassy areas of the Gorge. They are most active from March through early summer. All ticks are potential carriers of Rocky Mountain Spotted Fever. The western black-legged tick is responsible for transmitting Lyme Disease, a bacterial infection named for the Connecticut town where it was first recognized.

Your best defense against hosting a tick is to avoid areas infested with ticks and to wear clothing with a snug fit around the waist, wrists, and ankles. Wearing several layers of clothing is most effective in keeping ticks from reaching the body. Since ticks do not always bite right away (they often crawl around on a potential host for several hours before deciding where to feed on a victim's blood), a strong insect repellent can also be an effective deterrent against tick bites.

## POISON OAK

In addition to Oregon oak, the Gorge (especially the eastern part) is home to poison oak. In contact with skin, poison oak can cause an irritating rash which, although not life threatening, can ruin your outing. Resin produced by the plant cause redness, itching, and pain. The severity of the reaction varies, but the onset usually occurs within twelve hours of contact and can last for up to ten days.

Avoid contact with poison oak by learning to identify it. Remember: "Leaves of three, let it be."

Poison oak often sprouts leaflets in groups of three on woody, rust-colored stems. Leaves are shiny or dull green, turning red, orange, or brown in the fall. The leaves of poison oak are often heavily lobed around the edges.

To avoid contact, wear long pants and use care when choosing a cat hole. If you come into contact with poison oak, rinse the area immediately with lots of water, and if a rash develops apply calamine lotion to reduce itching.

## LIGHTNING

Do not be caught on a ridge or mountain top, under large or solitary trees, in the open, or near open water during a lightning storm. Try to seek shelter in a low-lying area—a dense stand of small, uniformly sized trees is ideal. Stay away from anything that might attract lightning, such as metal tent poles, graphite fishing rods, or pack frames.

## WATER

Few back country pleasures can top a cool drink from a high-country lake or stream. That refreshing drink of water along the trail is almost a tradition, but now, like other grand traditions, this one is fading away.

A protozoan called *Giardia lambia* has made this change permanent. This single-celled parasite, now found throughout the Columbia River Gorge and most other wild areas, causes severe intestinal disease.

All wilderness users must now take appropriate measures to insure water is pure by taking one of the following steps:

- Pack water from the faucet. (This can be difficult on long trips.)
- Rapidly boil water for at least ten minutes before drinking.
- Purify water with a filter. Ceramic or carbon based filtration systems are commonly sold in sporting goods stores.
- Add iodine tablets, drops, or other water purification tablets available at sporting goods stores.

Also, be aware of the source of your water. Snow melt, springs, and small intermittent streams are safer than large streams or lakes. Take all water upstream from the trail.

One final note: If you become ill about 2 to 4 weeks after your backcountry visit, see a physician immediately.

## CAR THEFT

Theft of property from unattended motor vehicles is becoming a significant problem in many areas—including the Gorge.

# 1  LEWIS & CLARK NATURE TRAIL

|  |  |
|---|---|
| **General description:** | A short day hike close to Portland with diverse flora. |
| **Distance:** | 3 miles round-trip. |
| **Difficulty:** | Easy. |
| **Trail type:** | Maintained. |
| **Traffic:** | Light. |
| **Best season:** | Year-round. |
| **Elevation gain:** | 50 feet. |
| **Maximum elevation:** | 150 feet. |
| **Topographic maps:** | Washougal USGS. |

**Finding the trailhead:** From Portland, take Interstate 84 east to the exit at the Lewis & Clark State Park just after the Troutdale exit. Follow the off ramp, then turn left under the railroad for 0.1 mile and then left again at Lewis & Clark State Park Rest Area. The trailhead is on the left side of the parking lot as you face the restrooms.

## LEWIS AND CLARK NATURE TRAIL

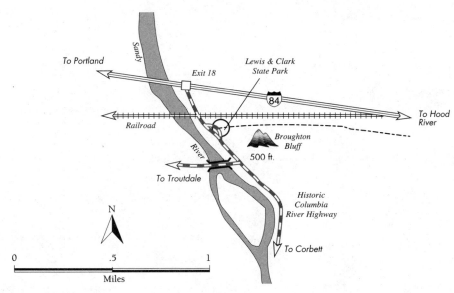

**Key points:**

**The trail:** I had to think hard about why I would hike this trail if I didn't want to cover all the gorge trails. Then it occurred to me that this trail is a good place to take your dog. This trail is not terribly scenic, or terribly quiet, thanks to Interstate 84 and the Union Pacific Railroad. It is billed by the interpretive trailhead sign as a good place to examine Oregon grape. The best examples of this common gorge plant are right beside the trailhead sign. The plants along the trail are those that thrive in wetter environments, such as knettles and cow parsnip.

 This is the nearest Gorge hike to the Portland metro area, and it is a good idea to get in the habit of not leaving valuables in your car. The Gorge trailheads receive a high volume of visitors, not all of whom are honest.

The trail follows the left fence from the parking lot, then at the end of the grassy picnic area the trail climbs slightly along Broughton Bluff, parallel to the interstate. The forest is primarily Oregon oak and big leaf maple, with several water loving western red cedars along the way. Be careful of nettles, which emit a chemical residue that causes severe itching with too much skin exposure. There are a few examples of Cascade Oregon grape, but it is not as common along this trail as some of the other Gorge trails like Elowah Falls.

The trail follows the north slope of Broughton Bluff for about 1.5 miles. You can turn around at any time and return to the trailhead via the same route.

|  |  |
|---|---|
| **General description:** | A short day hike above a nude beach—but you can't see much from the trail. |
| **Distance:** | 3 miles. |
| **Difficulty:** | Easy. |
| **Trail type:** | Maintained trail. |
| **Traffic:** | Light. |
| **Best season:** | Year-round. |
| **Elevation gain:** | 0 feet. |
| **Maximum elevation:** | 80 feet. |
| **Topographic maps:** | Bridal Veil Green Trails and Bridal Veil USGS. |

**Finding the trailhead:** From Portland, take Interstate 84 east to Rooster Rock State Park, exit 25. The off-ramp leads immediately to a toll booth for the park. The fee is $3.00, so read this entire description before choosing this hike. Turn right after paying and drive all the way to the end of the parking lots. The trail starts to the east, on the second trail above the beach entry.

## ROOSTER ROCK NATURE TRAIL

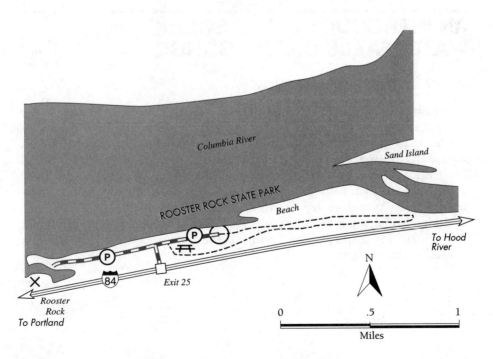

**Key points:**

1.3   Lookout
3.0   Trail ends in picnic sight A1

Special Regulations for Rooster Rock State Park:
1. Nudity is allowed 100 yards east of beach entry.

**The trail:** Lewis and Clark camped here April 6-9, 1806, on their return trip from the Pacific Ocean. They did not, from what I can gather from their journals, walk around naked, although they could have. The trail has many cobwebs, and I certainly don't suggest hiking naked. If you want to be naked, I suggest the beach. The path does not receive much traffic except for the occasional jogger.

The trail starts at the east end of the park, to the right of another trail leading into the trees. It stays in a thick forest of big leaf maple and cotton-wood, until it reaches a viewpoint of the interstate and up the Gorge. This is a unique perspective on the gorge, but not a good place to clear your head.

I recommend returning via the same route, because the rest of the loop is less pleasant. The return loop is closer to the interstate, used less frequently, and has more cobwebs. It terminates in group picnic site A1, near park headquarters. Hug the right edge of the lawn and cross a service road to the trailhead. It is another 0.2 mile to the other end of the lot where you parked. Have fun.

# AN INTRODUCTION TO SCENIC WATERFALLS OF THE GORGE

Because of the over 600–foot–thick layer of Columbia River basalt, the Gorge has over 30 waterfalls, most of which are within an hour's drive of Portland. To give you an introduction to the falls area, I suggest that you start with Latourell Falls, stop at the Falls at Shepperds Dell, and visit Bridal Veil Falls. It is easy to do all three in one day, even if you get up late. They are less visited than Multnomah Falls, but still receive heavy traffic. After-wards, if you have time, try the Multnomah Falls area.

Hiking Bridal Veil Falls, Shepperds Dell, Wahkeena Falls, and Multnomah Falls makes for a full day of hiking in the falls area along the Historic Columbia River Highway.

# 3 LATOURELL FALLS

| | |
|---|---|
| **General description:** | A short gentle hike to the falls. |
| **Distance:** | 2.1 miles. |
| **Difficulty:** | Easy. |
| **Trail type:** | Well-maintained. |
| **Traffic:** | Heavy. |
| **Best season:** | Year-round. |
| **Elevation gain:** | 610 feet. |
| **Maximum elevation:** | 900 feet. |
| **Topographic maps:** | Bridal Veil Green Trails, Bridal Veil USGS. |

**Finding the trailhead:** From Portland, take Interstate 84 east to Bridal Veil Exit 28. Follow the off-ramp to the intersection with the Historic Columbia River Highway. Turn right and head west for 2.8 miles to the Latourell Falls Trailhead. Park on the left. A paved trail starts on the south side of the parking lot. Bathrooms are available on the north side of the road by the bridge.

## Key points:

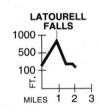

0.2   Latourell Falls Lookout (end of pavement)
0.5   Junction with the cutoff trail where you
      can shorten the loop
1.0   Upper Latourell Falls
1.5   Junction with other side of cutoff trail
2.1   Return to highway west of trailhead

**The trail:** This trail is an easy hike and a good introduction to the waterfalls of the area. You have good views of upper and lower Latourell Falls. The lower falls is 220 feet tall, and even if it is not a large volume of water, the height makes Latourell Falls spectacular.

From the trailhead on the southeast side of the parking area, follow a paved path up to a lookout below lower Latourell Falls. The pavement ends shortly after the lookout, and a well-used dirt path begins. The trail climbs steeply up above the falls, with devil's club and lady ferns along the way. Then after climbing about 300 feet, the trail flattens out.

At 0.5 mile, you reach the junction with the cutoff trail to the return loop on the other side of Latourell Creek. Stay left, heading south, to see the upper falls. The trail continues at a gentle grade through cedar forest. Western red cedar trees are very shade tolerant and do not require a lot of sunlight, but they do need a lot of water. You cross several footbridges before reaching the upper falls.

At Upper Latourell Falls the bridge crosses the stream just below the falls. You can take a short path on the opposite side of the creek, underneath the falls, but the rock is slippery and wet.

# LATOURELL FALLS

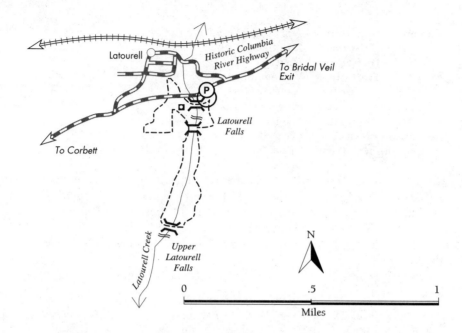

 Waterfalls in the Gorge receive many visitors, and staying on the trail helps keep each waterfall just as it was the last time someone visited it.

Past the falls, the trail continues to be level and turns down north, to the other side, to reach the cutoff trail. Stay left for the scenic highway and several lookout spots with benches for a moment of silence. There is a slight climb to the lookouts, then the trail drops on switchbacks past one of my favorite bigleaf maple trees. Bent into a "u" shape over the trail, it is easy to walk underneath. This is one way for a tree to capitalize on the sunlight left by the cleared trail, without getting in the way of the trail crew.

After 2.1 miles, the trail returns to the Gorge Scenic Highway on the west side of the bridge over Latourell Creek. It is a 0.2 mile walk back to the trailhead. If you are not too tired, and you're anxious to see more waterfalls, drive east on the highway to Shepperds Dell, Bridal Veil, and beyond.

## LOWER FALLS TRAIL

There is also a paved nature path leading below the lower falls. It leaves the parking lot on the south side of the highway, just before the bridge over Latourell Creek. It enables you to look up at the misty crash of water and get some good pictures. If you follow the lower trail from the parking lot, it will take you along Latourell Creek to Guy W. Talbot State Park, but as the trail does not loop back to the parking lot at Latourell Falls, I suggest returning via the same route back to the trailhead.

# 4  FALLS AT SHEPPERDS DELL

| | |
|---|---|
| **General description:** | A very short walk into Shepperds Dell above the falls. |
| **Distance:** | 0.2 mile. |
| **Difficulty:** | Easy. |
| **Traffic:** | Heavy. |
| **Trail type:** | Well-maintained. |
| **Best season:** | Year-round. |
| **Elevation gain:** | -20 feet. |
| **Maximum elevation:** | 260 feet. |
| **Topographic maps:** | Bridal Veil Green Trails, Bridal Veil USGS. |

**Finding the trailhead:** From Portland, take Interstate 84 east to Bridal Veil Exit 28. Follow the off-ramp to the intersection with the Historic Columbia River Highway. Turn right and travel 1.7 miles to the pullouts on either side of the highway just before the bridge over Shepperds Dell. The trailhead is a staircase before the bridge on the south side. No bathrooms are available, but there are bathrooms 1 mile west at Latourell Falls.

**Key points:**

0.1   Falls at Shepperds Dell Lookout

**The trail:** This is an easy hike that only takes about 15 minutes, leaving you with plenty of time to gaze in wonderment at the series of cascades inside a rock-sheltered cove. Don't plan to make this hike your sole destination, but it is a good stop after hiking Latourell or Bridal Veil.

This trail begins its descent on a brief staircase. The trail winds around the sheer basalt rock face of the dell to a guardrailed lookout above the falls.

# FALLS AT SHEPPERDS DELL

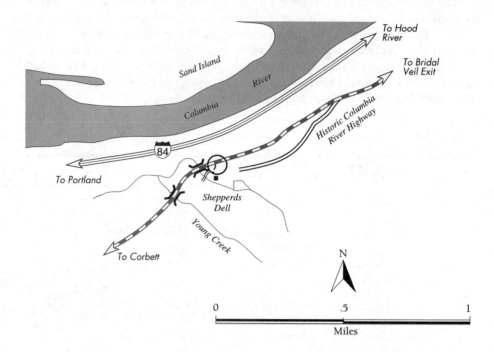

Shepperds Dell is surrounded by rock on all three sides except for the gateway to the Columbia River necessary for drainage. Looking underneath the bridge gives you a feel for the height and erosive power of the rushing water that carved this dell.

Return via the same path and enjoy another falls area hike.

# 5    BRIDAL VEIL FALLS AND
        OVERLOOK LOOP TRAIL

| | |
|---|---|
| **General description:** | A short 0.7 mile walk to an overlook above Bridal Veil Falls with a nature trail option afterwards. |
| **Distance:** | 1.1 miles. |
| **Difficulty:** | Easy. |
| **Traffic:** | Heavy. |
| **Trail type:** | Well-maintained. |
| **Best season:** | Year-round. |
| **Elevation gain:** | -50 feet. |
| **Maximum elevation:** | 250 feet. |
| **Topographic maps:** | Bridal Veil Green Trails, Bridal Veil USGS. |

**Finding the trailhead:** From Portland, take Interstate 84 east to Bridal Veil Exit 28. Follow the off-ramp to the intersection with the Historic Columbia River Highway. Turn right and travel 0.8 mile and the trailhead will be on the right, just after crossing Bridal Veil Creek. Turn into the parking lot and the trailhead is on the east end, near the bathrooms.

## BRIDAL VEIL

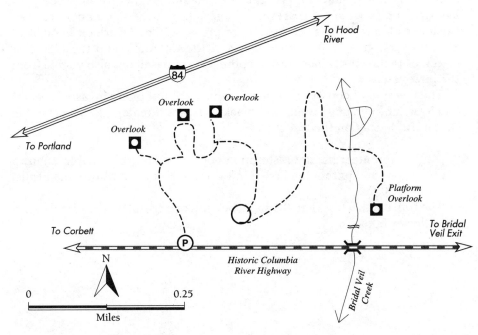

**Key points:**

- 0.1 Junction with unmarked trail that dead ends, stay left.
- 0.3 Bridal Veil Lookout.
- 0.6 Return to trailhead.
- 1.1 Return to parking lot after loop trail.

**The trail:** The trail is an easy hike above one of the more nameworthy falls in the area. The water demands of the logging industry and the reservoir above the falls used to reduce the falls to a trickle in late season, but the mill is no longer here and only its remnants are visible. Bridal Veil Falls is there every day for your enjoyment.

At the trailhead the path splits in two. Stay right, heading east, for the falls. The left fork becomes a nature trail that makes a nice walk after returning from the falls. Soon the pavement ends and the often muddy trail leads into the deciduous forest toward the falls.

At 0.1 mile, the trail comes to an unmarked intersection that often confuses hikers. Do not take the right trail to the south—it was a bushwhacker's attempt to reach the top of the falls. Stay left, heading east, and descend on a switchback to the bridge across the creek. Once across the creek, the trail leads to a wooden staircase and lookout below the falls. The large basalt rocks on which the platform is built offer a good foreground object for photographing the falls.

Return via the same trail to the trailhead.

---

## OVERLOOK LOOP OPTION

At the trailhead junction take the left trail and head north. A paved path leads out onto the small plateau. A large interpretive sign announces the existence of camas lilies on this nature preserve. The Overlook Loop Trail offers several good lookouts for views of the Columbia and the Pillars of Hercules to the west. These eroded pinnacles of basalt are also visible from the interstate.

The Overlook Loop Trail has some camas lily, but many invasive species like Scotch broom and Himalayan blackberry are threatening this preserve. Be careful to stay on the trail.

 Volunteer habitat restoration opportunities are available. Inquire at the Multnomah Lodge Information Center at Multnomah Falls.

The trail ends in less than 0.5 mile, but you can spend plenty of time with your flower book.

# 6 COOPEY FALLS AND ANGELS REST WITH DEVILS REST LOOP OPTION

| | |
|---|---|
| **General description:** | A short, gentle hike to the falls, an intermediate hike to Angels Rest Lookout for a view, and a long day hike to Devils Rest for more views. |
| **Distance:** | 4.4 miles, 10.8 if you take the Devils Rest Loop option. |
| **Difficulty:** | Easy to Coopey Falls, intermediate to Angels Rest, and difficult to Devils Rest. |
| **Traffic:** | Moderate. |
| **Trail type:** | Well-maintained, with a primitive hiking section on Devils Rest Loop. |
| **Best season:** | Year–round, depending upon frost line. Try Devils Rest May through October. |
| **Elevation gain:** | 1,540 feet to Angels Rest. |
| **Maximum elevation:** | 1,640 feet. |
| **Topographic maps:** | Bridal Veil Green Trails and Bridal Veil USGS. |

**Finding the trailhead:** From Portland, take Interstate 84 east to Bridal Veil Exit 28. Follow the off-ramp to the intersection with the Historic Columbia River Highway and park to the right in a dirt lot. Angels Rest Trail 415 starts across the highway to the south.

## Key points:
- 0.8   Coopey Falls lookouts
- 2.2   Angels Rest Lookout Trail

## Devils Rest Loop Option:
- 2.3   Junction with Fox Glove Trail
- 4.9   Junction with Wahkeena Trail 420
- 5.2   Junciton with Devils Rest Trail 420C
- 7.8   Devils Rest
- 8.6   Junction with Fox Glove Trail
- 9.6   Return to Angels Rest Trail 415

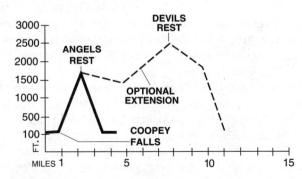

# COOPEY FALLS AND ANGELS REST

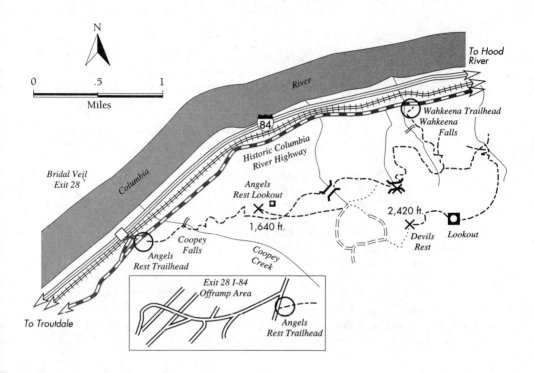

**The trail:** This trail is a good hike for people who don't want a really steep climb, but don't mind getting a little exercise. The views from Angels Rest are superb and the trail up is gradual. This trail also offers a chance to see the forest recovering from the 1991 fire that burned these hills; many salmonberry and thimbleberry plants thrive in the open space left by the fire. Several loop options are available from this trailhead. They require a shuttle to Wahkeena or a longer trip back from Devils Rest.

From the trailhead, Trail 415 climbs gradually, winding through forest into open slide areas. Burn marks are evident on many of the older trees that survived the fire. A recent burn allows sunlight to reach the forest floor, fostering the growth of lots of bushy plants like ocean spray, thimbleberry, and wildflowers.

At 0.8 mile you reach Coopey Falls. There are several spur lookout trails to the left for views down onto the crashing waters of the falls. After the falls, bear right. The trail crosses the creek on a footbridge and climbs more steadily into the shade, then takes long switchbacks up another burn area with thick underbrush. The trail climbs right to the base of Angels Rest before veering south on one last long, gentle switchback up to the top. On the last stretch the trail crosses a rocky section where the trail seems to disappear. Look straight ahead for the trail, not uphill. It continues across flat rocks.

At 2.2 miles you reach a junction before going out onto Angels Rest. To your right, heading east, is the continuation of Trail 415 to the Wahkeena area and Devils Rest. The left trail, heading north, is a lookout spur which extends all the way out to the end of Angels Rest, a prominent, flat, cliff-sided point. From the interstate it looks like it would make a perfect heli-copter landing pad. It is covered partially by bushes and large rocks, but offers excellent views and some good lunch-spot rocks.

You can return to your car via the same trail or hike to Devils Rest or Wahkeena Trail. A trip to Wahkeena requires a shuttle car at the Multnomah Falls or Wahkeena trailheads.

---

## DEVILS REST LOOP OPTION/WAHKEENA LOOP OPTION

 The Devils Rest Loop option requires good route-finding skills. If you aren't comfortable with your map and compass skills, consider a trip to Wahkeena instead.

At the junction with the spur trail out onto Angels Rest, turn right, head-ing east; the trail climbs gently up one switchback. Next, watch for a trail forking to the left at 2.3 miles—this is the main trail. Straight ahead is the Fox Glove Trail Area. Stay left, continuing east on Trail 415 for Wahkeena and Devils Rest. You can reach Devils Rest by going right, but the trail is harder to follow.

Trail 415 follows along the rim of the ridge. Through the trees you can get a view of Angels Rest with the lower Columbia below. The trail crosses several small footbridges as it winds along through large Douglas–firs and an understory less dense than in the burned area. After crossing a third creek on a footbridge, the trail begins to make gentle switchbacks down-ward. Some trees here survived the 1991 fire and have a competitive advan-tage over the bushy plants.

At 4.8 miles, the trail flattens out, climbing slightly. After crossing Wahkeena Spring on a footbridge you will reach the junction with Wahkeena Trail 420. Turn left, heading north, for the Wahkeena Trailhead, stay right, continuing east for Devils Rest on what is now Trail 420 also. Taking the trail to Wahkeena is a good option for less experienced hikers.

Trail 420 begins to climb steadily for 0.4 mile to the junction with the Vista Point Trail 419. Several old stone trail markers lie around a pile of rocks that forms the junction. About 30 feet past this junction to the east the Devils Rest Trail 420C veers right, turning south.

After taking the Devils Rest Trail 420C just past the junction, the trail climbs steep switchbacks for 0.5 mile before flattening out onto the narrow plateau toward Devils Rest. One unmarked trail veers left, but stay right as the trail curves west. Then an old road intersects with the main trail—keep

*The 1991 burn below Angels Rest.*

bearing right to the west. There are two good viewpoints on the way to Devils Rest—the first, on a large rock, offers views of everything north of the river, including Table Mountain and Hamilton Mountain. The second lookout requires a short walk out to get a peek at the Gorge. Continue past the lookouts to Devils Rest.

Devils Rest is a good place for a rest, but does not offer as good a view as the previous lookouts, since it is tree covered. Look for an unmarked trail on the left that continues past the end of Trail 420C, the one you arrived on. This route to the west is faint and at times difficult to follow, but it offers a shortcut back to the Angels Rest Trail 415.

 When following a faint trail look for cairns, cut logs, blazes, and sometimes, flagging.

Follow this trail through a young stand of trees with various stumps along the way. After less than 0.5 mile, the trail comes to an old logging road; going either right or left will take you back to the Fox Glove Trail. If you choose left, bear right past two junctions until you reach the marked junction with the Fox Glove Trail, then turn left.

Going right, or continuing slightly more northward on the old road, will take you to an old log staging area. Once on the other side of it, follow a faint trail to the north through blown down Oregon oak to another old road, then turn left, heading west, cross a small creek, and hike another 0.1 mile to the junction with Fox Glove Trail. Turn right, continuing west, onto Fox Glove Trail for Angels Rest.

The Fox Glove winds through shady forest before rejoining Trail 415 back to Angels Rest. Follow the main trail back to the Angels Rest Trailhead.

# MULTNOMAH FALLS RECREATION AREA

**Overview:**

Multnomah Falls is the best known and most visited spot in the Columbia River Gorge National Scenic Area. It receives over two million visitors per year and has its own exit off of Interstate 84. At the base of the falls, Multnomah Falls Lodge was constructed in 1925. It contains a restaurant, gift shop, Forest Service Visitor Center, and various concessions selling hot dogs, coffee, and ice cream.

Because Multnomah Falls receives such heavy use and is a national landmark besides, groups like the Friends of Multnomah Falls were created to insure its preservation. The interpretive center relies heavily on volunteers for its staff. If you would like more information on how you can help Multnomah Falls, and on attending events sponsored by the Friends of Multnomah Falls, please contact:

Friends of Multnomah Falls or Multnomah Falls Interpretive Center
P. O. Box 426                 503-695-2372
Troutdale, OR 97069
503-761-4751

Besides this volunteer help, the scenic area staff has begun to manage the falls more like an urban park, with trail patrols to monitor switchback cutting and other problems. The scenic area is closed at night, and all off–trail activity is prohibited. One might ask how the wilderness experience is maintained. Well, it is not a *wilderness* experience to hike to Multnomah Falls, but it is a *natural* experience. No matter what conditions exist on the trail, in the parking lot, and at the top, Multnomah Falls keeps crashing down, and everyone gets to see, enjoy, and tell their friends about it.

You must hike this area differntly than you would other areas in the Gorge. To avoid crowds, try the Wahkeena Loop. It is heavily used, but does not receive nearly as many visitors as the main trail to the Falls. However, the main 1.1 mile route at the Falls is the shortest, fastest way to get to the top, look down, and come back, so if all you want to do is see this famous landmark from the best angle, choose the Multnomah Falls Hike. Although you could make the Wahkeena Loop an overnight trip, the best backpacking trip in the area is the Larch Mountain Trail, which does include a trip to the Falls, plus the several falls above. If you want to visit Larch Mountain without hiking to the top, try the Larch Mountain Loop or Sherrard Point hikes. Larch Mountain Loop offers pretty easy overnight opportunities for camping. Either way, Multnomah Falls is the stuff. Happy hiking.

## Special Regulations for Multnomah Falls

1. Off–trail travel prohibited.
2. Pets on a 6–foot leash only.
3. Upper Plunge Pool closed.
4. Trail closes from dusk till dawn.
5. Camping is permitted 0.5 mile past the top of the falls.
6. Climbing and other activities on the face of the falls are prohibited.

# 7    MULTNOMAH FALLS

**Note:** A 1998 slide and the resultant unstable slope between the Benson Bridge and the junction with Trail 400 made a hike on Trail 441 from the visitor center to the falls temporarily impossible. Check with the visitor center before planning to hike the falls. The USDAFS plans to reroute or rebuild the trail as soon as the area is safe and an alternative trail can be approved. You can still access the Multnomah Falls overlook and Larch Mountain via the Oneonta Trailhead and Trail 400, but the USDAFS encourages visitors to explore other areas of the Gorge until the problem is resolved.

| | |
|---|---|
| **General description:** | The premier Columbia Gorge hike. |
| **Distance:** | 2.2 miles. |
| **Difficulty:** | Moderate (short and easy to follow, but uphill all the way). |
| **Traffic:** | Very heavy. |
| **Trail type:** | Well-maintained. |
| **Best season:** | May through October. |
| **Elevation gain:** | 700 feet. |
| **Maximum elevation:** | 800 feet. |
| **Topographic maps:** | Multnomah Falls USGS or Bridal Veil Green Trails. |

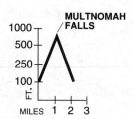

**Finding the trailhead:** From Portland, drive east on Interstate 84 to Exit 31 for Multnomah Falls. Park, and walk south, underneath the interstate and the train tracks, to the Multnomah Falls Lodge and

# MULTNOMAH FALLS AND WAHKEENA LOOP

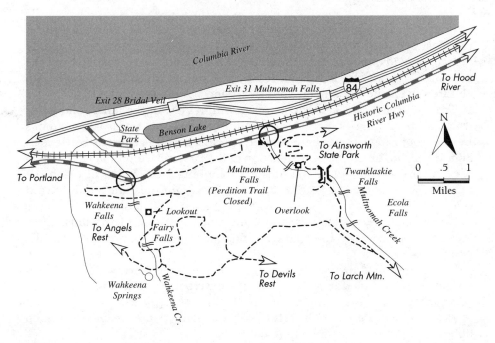

Visitor Center. Trail 441 starts east of the lodge on a cement staircase. Multnomah Falls is visible from the highway and the parking area.

You can also reach the trailhead by taking Bridal Veil Exit 28, 3 miles before the Multnomah Falls exit. This allows you the flexibility to try other falls hikes in the area, like Latourell and Wahkeena.

### Key points:
    0.3    Junction with Gorge Trail 400
    1.0    Junction with lookout trail above falls
    1.1    Overlook
    2.2    Return to trailhead

**The trail:** If you don't like crowds, please avoid Multnomah Falls—but first consider that Multnomah Falls is a national treasure. It is almost your duty as a visitor to the Columbia River Gorge to hike to the top at least once. At over 620 feet high, Multnomah Falls is the highest falls in the Gorge and perhaps the most spectacular. Ira Williams put it best when describing Multnomah Falls:

Long have its praises been sung, and as our familiarity and knowledge of its idiosyncrasies grow, we come to realize that only the sweetest of strains can begin to express the love and reverence that this pygmy-giant but master stroke of Nature's busy hand must stir in every open heart. The rush of its waters is music that enthralls and its picturesque surroundings beyond the skill of the artist's brush to portray.

From this description it is easy to understand why Multnomah Falls is the most popular hike in the Gorge. All that you need is patience, a friendly demeanor, and about an hour. It is easy to reach and clearly visible from the interstate. Where else is there a 1.2-mile-long paved trail for people with children in strollers? So open your heart and have a good hike.

The trail starts on a cement staircase within view of the falls. Follow this trail, the beginning of Larch Mountain Trail 441, up toward the famous Benson Footbridge. It was named after a prominent and generous Portlander, Simon Benson, during the construction of the Historic Columbia River Highway. After crossing below the falls and climbing a bit, you will reach the junction with Gorge Trail 400 at 0.3 mile. Stay right, heading south toward the top.

The asphalt path switchbacks up the slope just east of the falls. After cresting a slight ridge, the trail descends quickly to the junction with the lookout trail.

Turn right, heading west, to view the falls. After a short walk, you reach a steel and wood platform. The railing is for resource protection as well as your safety.

Have a good stare. Then, return via the same route or choose a loop option like the Wahkeena Loop (Hike 8).

# 8  WAHKEENA LOOP WITH DEVILS REST OPTION

See Map on Page 33

|  |  |
|---|---|
| **General description:** | A popular day hike offering views of several famous Columbia Gorge waterfalls in the Multnomah Falls area. |
| **Distance:** | 5.7 miles |
| **Difficulty:** | Intermediate. |
| **Traffic:** | Heavy. |
| **Trail type:** | Well- maintained. |
| **Best season:** | Year-round. |
| **Elevation gain:** | 1,500 feet. |
| **Maximum elevation:** | 1,600 feet. |
| **Topographic maps:** | Bridal Veil Green Trails, Bridal Veil and Multnomah Falls USGS. |

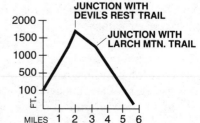

**Finding the trailhead:** From Portland, take Interstate 84 east to Bridal Veil Exit 28. Follow the off-ramp and then turn left onto the Columbia Gorge Highway; drive 2.5 miles to the Wahkeena picnic area and trailhead. The trail starts on the right. Bathrooms are available at the Multnomah Falls Lodge, 0.5 mile     further. I recommend parking at Wahkeena to complete the loop back to Multnomah Falls, because parking is usually easier to find here. Wahkeena has restrooms in the picnic area, which are open during summer season.

**Key points:**

| | |
|---|---|
| 0.4 | Old Perdition Trail 421 |
| 1.2 | Vista Point Trail 419 |
| 1.6 | Angels Rest Trail 415 |
| 2.0 | Vista Point Trail 419 rejoins main trail |
| 3.2 | Larch Mountain Trail 441 |
| 3.9 | Old Perdition Trail 421  rejoins main trail |
| 4.0 | Multnomah Falls Viewpoint Trail |
| 5.0 | Multnomah Falls Lodge |
| 5.7 | Wahkeena Trailhead |

**The trail:** This is a pleasant alternative to just walking up to Multnomah Falls and back again. You can do the loop either way, but I suggest going up Wahkeena first.

Wahkeena Trail 420 climbs steadily from the start. The path is wide past several switchbacks and old slides. A stone bridge just below Wahkeena Falls makes for a misty rest spot. In the winter, if the temperature gets below freezing, the bridge becomes a sheet of ice and is practically impassable.

 The Gorge waterfalls are especially pretty when the spray is frozen and skirted by ice sculpture.

Just after the bridge is the junction with the Old Perdition Trail 421. Perdition Trail 421 was closed indefinitely after the 1991 fire and the 1996 slides. Stay right, heading south, because entering a closed area is illegal and unsafe.

Next is the junction with two lookout trails. The more heavily used trail on the right leads out to Lemmon's Viewpoint. It offers significant views across the mile-wide Columbia. The left spur, to the south, makes an abrupt climb on an unmaintained trail for 0.3 mile to Monument Viewpoint.

Once back on the main trail, climb to Fairy Falls, a small cascade in a cool glen. A cedar log bench offers an opportunity for relaxation and contemplation.

At 1.2 miles up the Wahkeena Trail 420 is the Vista Point junction with Trail 419. If you don't take the Vista Point route, you won't miss much. The views from Lemmon's Viewpoint are much better. If you do choose to follow the Vista Point Trail you may end up wondering where Vista Point was. Vista Point is only a spur trail that veers off to the left of Trail 419 at an unmarked junction, at the end of a flat bend. Fire-scarred trees provide enough of an opening for a simple view across the Gorge.

I suggest keeping to your right and continuing south on the Wahkeena Trail 420. It is cooler, and the rushing water drowns out highway sounds. At 1.8 miles is the Angels Rest Trail 415; stay left, heading east, for Multnomah Falls. Trail 415 to your right takes you past Wahkeena Springs toward Angels Rest and longer hiking options. (See the Angels Rest Hike.) The trail climbs some more before it is rejoined by the Vista Point Trail 419.

The junction consists of old stone trail markers that may not point you in the right direction if followed. Continue straight, heading east, for Multnomah Falls and the Larch Mountain Trail. Just 30 feet east of the junction with Trail 419 is another junction with the Trail 420C to Devils Rest. Stay left, continuing east. (To hike to Devils Rest instead, turn up this trail and follow Devil Rest Option below.)

After a 0.5 mile descent you reach the junction with Larch Mountain 441. Continue 3.2 miles in and turn left, heading north, to see a couple of 80–foot waterfalls (Ecola and Twanklaskie) down Multnomah Creek. The two upper falls below the junction with the Wahkeena Trail 420 receive fewer visitors than Multnomah Falls, despite their close proximity; hence they offer a less crowded perspective on this famous area.

Before crossing the bridge to the Multnomah Lookout Trail junction you reach the intersection with the closed Perdition Trail 421. Again stay to your right, avoiding the closure.

*Hikers below Wahkeena Falls*

After crossing Multnomah Creek on the bridge, try a spur trail left, to the west, as the trail turns to pavement, where you can get a look at Multnomah Falls. From the lookout you can see down to your destination, the historic Multnomah Falls Lodge. Once back on Trail 441 heading north, climb a couple of hundred feet on the paved path. The final descent is on the crowded Multnomah Falls Trail. Next, stay left, continuing north, at the intersection with Gorge Trail 400.

After decending to Multnomah Falls Lodge, turn west and walk on the road for a short distance. When the road narrows, look for a well–marked path on the uphill side. Take this return trail back to your parked car at Wahkeena Trailhead.

### DEVILS REST OPTION

Just past Vista Point junction with the Wahkeena Trail, turn right, heading south and up along the Devils Rest Trail 420C. After the junction, the trail climbs steep switchbacks for 0.5 mile before flattening out onto the narrow plateau leading to Devils Rest. One unmarked trail veers left; stay right. Then an old road intersects with the main trail—stay right again. There are two viewpoints on the way to Devils Rest: the first, on a large rock, offers views of everything north of the Gorge, including Table Mountain and Hamilton Mountain. The second lookout requires a short walk out to get a peek at the gorge.

Devil's Rest is a good place for a rest, but does not offer a view, as it is tree–covered. Return via Trail 420C to finish the Wahkeena Loop hike.

## 9    LARCH MOUNTAIN FROM MULTNOMAH FALLS

| | |
|---|---|
| General description: | A premier Columbia Gorge hike with spectacular waterfalls, old growth forest, and clear, clean Multnomah Creek. |
| Distance: | 7 miles. |
| Difficulty: | Difficult. |
| Traffic: | Heavy to moderate. |
| Trail type: | Well-maintained. |
| Best season: | May through October. |
| Elevation gain: | 3,840 feet. |
| Maximum elevation: | 3,940 feet. |
| Topographic maps: | Bridal Veil USGS, Bridal Veil Green Trails. |

**Finding the trailhead:** From Portland, drive east on Interstate 84 to Exit 31 for Multnomah Falls. Park and walk south, underneath the interstate and the train tracks, to the Multnomah Falls Lodge and Visitor Center. The trail begins west of the lodge on a cement staircase. Multnomah Falls is visible from the highway and the parking area.

You can also reach the trailhead by taking the Bridal Veil exit (Exit 28), 3 miles before the Multnomah Falls exit. This allows you more freedom to do other falls hikes in the area, like Latourell and Wahkeena.

To hike one-way to Larch Mountain, leave a car at the top. From Portland, take Interstate 84 east just past Troutdale and take Exit 18 for Lewis & Clark State Park. Follow the off-ramp until it ends at Crown Point Highway, then turn left and follow the main road to Corbett. Two miles past Corbett, the road forks near Women's Forum Viewpoint, which offers a good view of the Vista House and Larch Mountain. Turn right, continuing east, at the fork onto Larch Mountain Road. Fourteen miles of pretty, paved, and winding road later is the Larch Mountain Trailhead.

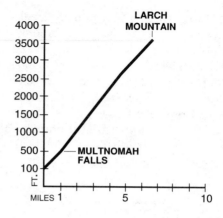

**Key points:**

| | |
|---|---|
| 0.3 | Junction with Gorge Trail 400 |
| 1.0 | Junction with lookout trail above falls |
| 1.1 | Junction with the Old Perdition Trail 421 |
| 1.8 | Junction with the Wahkeena Trail 420 |
| 3.0 | Junction with Franklin Ridge Trail 427 |
| 4.8 | Junction with Multnomah Creek Way 444 |
| 5.3 | Junction with jeep road |
| 6.8 | Larch Mountain Trailhead |

**The trail:** If you do not like crowds, please avoid Multnomah Falls. Past Multnomah Falls, however, the Larch Mountain Trail is not as crowded and the route follows cool, clear Multnomah Creek. The hike is easier going uphill because there are a few flat spots to rest your downhill knees. Twanlaskie and Ecola Falls, past Multnomah, also provide additional scenery on the extended route. There is not much of a view after the Multnomah Falls lookout, until the Sherrard Point option on the top of Larch Mountain.

Larch Mountain Trail 441 starts on a cement staircase within view of the falls. Follow this up toward the famous Benson footbridge, named after Simon Benson. It was built in 1915 and is one of the first continuously poured concrete structures in the United States. Benson was a prominent lumberman and generous Portlander during the construction of the Historic Columbia River Highway. He gave this land to the City of Portland as a park and it was later transferred to the USFS. After crossing below the falls, and climbing a bit, at 0.3 mile you reach the junction with Gorge Trail 400. Stay right, heading south toward the top.

The asphalt path switchbacks up the slope just east of the falls. After cresting a slight ridge, the trail descends quickly to the junction with the

# LARCH MOUNTAIN

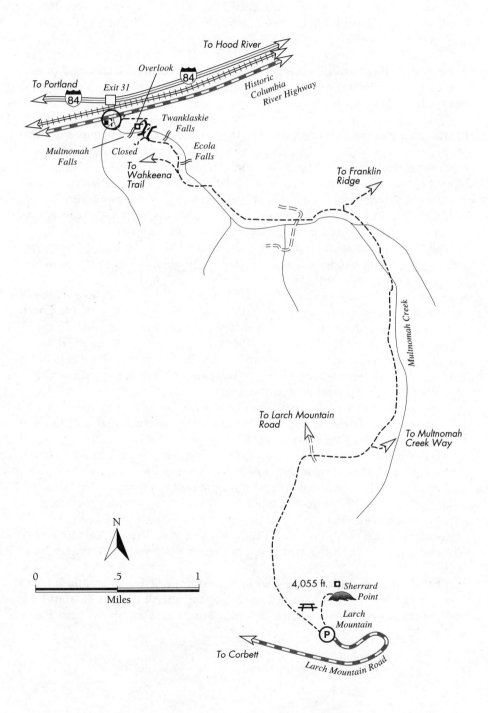

To Hood River

Overlook

84

To Portland

Exit 31

84

Historic
Columbia
River Highway

Twanklaskie
Falls

Multnomah
Falls

Closed

Ecola
Falls

To
Wahkeena
Trail

To Franklin
Ridge

Multnomah Creek

To Larch Mountain
Road

To Multnomah
Creek Way

N

0          .5          1

Miles

4,055 ft.   Sherrard
Point

Larch
Mountain

P

To Corbett

Larch Mountain Road

lookout trail.

Once back on the main trail, if you are not too tired, cross the bridge over Multnomah Creek, heading south. Stay left, continuing south past the old Perdition Trail 421, which has been closed indefinitely thanks to the fire in 1991 and the flooding in 1996.

The trail climbs steadily to Twanklaskie Falls, which has a nice pool but a short drop. Further up is the Ecola Falls, which drops further and makes a bigger splash. Neither of the upper falls are as spectacular as Multnomah, but each has its own beauty.

At 1.8 miles is the junction with Wahkeena Trail 420. This section is one of the most photogenic, with moving water, large rocks, and mosses. (The Wahkeena loop option is described in the Wahkeena Loop Hike.) Stay left, continuing south, toward Larch Mountain. Cross the bridge over Multnomah Creek; a campsite is located up on the left 0.2 mile past the bridge. It has room for 1-2 tents and water is relatively close by. There is another campsite with 1-2 tent sites opposite several cascades on the basalt wall across the creek. It makes for a pleasant overnight or picnic spot.

Trail 441 is cool even on a hot day. It climbs above the basalt layers into more gravelly sandstone bands. The creek is filled with big, round boulders and the forest is mostly deciduous.

At 3.0 miles is a junction with the Franklin Ridge Trail 427, which is maintained but not heavily used. Stay right, continuing south, for Larch Mountain. Next, after crossing a log bridge over the east fork of Multnomah Creek, is a campsite by the river on the opposite bank to the west. It offers 2-3 tent sites, a fire ring, and plenty of water. Then, at 0.1 mile further, before crossing a second log bridge, you'll find another camp with multiple tent sites, a fire ring, and easy water access.

Next, pass a rock–slide area into old growth Douglas–firs and hemlock trees up to 6 feet in diameter. At 4.8 miles is the junction with Multnomah Creek Way 444, stay right coninuting south of Trail 441.

At 5.3 miles the trail crosses an old logging road, which leads to Larch Mountain Road. Just before the junction is a primitive campsite in a grove of large trees. There is a fire pit and multiple tent sites, but no immediately available water. (Water is available 0.7 mile back, at the junction with Multnomah Creek Way.)

Once past the road, the trail offers few views of the surrounding area. The last leg of the climb is through a dense forest of young mountain hemlock.

There is not much of a view from the summit of Larch Mountain, but you can take the Sherrard Point hike out to the site of the old lookout for a view of the main Cascades, with Mounts Rainier, St. Helen's, Adams, Hood, and Jefferson all in a line.

| | |
|---|---|
| **General description:** | A fairly easy loop walk in the heavily forested Larch Mountain area. |
| **Distance:** | 6 miles. |
| **Difficulty:** | Moderate. |
| **Traffic:** | Moderate. |
| **Trail type:** | Well-maintained. |
| **Best season:** | May to October. |
| **Elevation gain:** | 1,220 feet. |
| **Maximum elevation:** | 3,940 feet. |
| **Topographic maps:** | Bridal Veil USGS, Bridal Veil Green Trails. |

**Finding the trailhead:** From Portland, take Interstate 84 east just past Troutdale and take Exit 18 for Lewis & Clark State Park. Follow the off-ramp until it ends at the Crown Point Highway and turn left, heading south. Follow the scenic highway through Corbett. Two miles past Corbett the road forks; make a right onto Larch Mountain Road. Fourteen miles of pretty, paved, and winding road later is the Larch Mountain Trailhead.

**Key points:**
- 1.5    Junction with Jeep Trail to Larch Mountain Road
- 2.0    Multnomah Creek Way Trail 444
- 2.2    Multnomah Spur Trail 446
- 3.0    Oneonta Trail 424
- 3.8    Bell Creek Trail 459
- 4.8    Multnomah Creek Way Trail 444
- 5.7    Larch Mountain Road
- 6.0    Larch Mountain Trailhead

**The Trail:** Larch Mountain Trail is one of the few Gorge trails open to mountain bikes. Stay alert for other users. While you are at the top, I suggest a quick walk out to Sherrard Point which is 0.2 mile from the parking lot. The trail to Sherrard Point is described in the Sherrard Point Hike. It is just a short walk from the summit.

The Larch Mountain Trail starts just to the left of the bathrooms. It doesn't offer much in the way of views of the surrounding area, but it can be peaceful. From the top, the trail passes through the picnic area and past several cutoff trails joining the main trail. Keep going straight, heading north.

After 1.5 miles, the trail crosses an old logging road, which is now a popu-

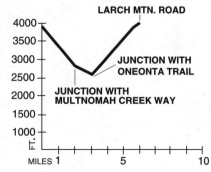

lar shortcut to Larch Mountain Road. Just after the junction is a primitive campsite in a grove of large hemlocks and firs. There is no water, but there is a fire pit and multiple tent sites. Water is available 0.7 miles further near the junction of Multnomah Creek Way with the main trail.

Two miles further down the trail is the junction with Multnomah Creek Way 444, which gives you three loop options. The longest continues down the Larch Mountain Trail to the Franklin Ridge Trail 427 and follows Multnomah Creek through some pretty cascades and rock gardens. It is 4.3 miles longer, and the Franklin Ridge Trail 427 back is not very scenic.

For the two shorter loops turn right, heading east, on Multnomah Creek Way 444. After 0.2 mile through increasingly lush vegetation, cross Multnomah Creek. At the crossing is a campsite with room for 2-3 tents, a fire ring, and water access.

Across the stream, at the junction with the Multnomah Spur Trail 446, you can choose to go right or left. Both trails end up connecting with the Oneonta Trail 424 back to the top and are about the same distance. I recommend the left one because of the additional campsite at the next water crossing and the presence of serious old growth cedars there.

On the left trail continuing east, the Multnomah Spur Trail 446 is relatively flat and in the trees. There are more water–loving cedars here and less fir. Another 0.25 mile further on the Multnomah Spur is another camp. One tent site, a fire pit, and water access await.

At 3 miles is the junction with Oneonta Trail 424. This shady spot, surrounded by giant firs, is a great place for a nap. After dozing for a bit and drinking some water, turn right, heading southwest, for the climb back up Oneonta Trail 424.

At 3.8 miles, the Bell Creek Trail 459 joins the Oneonta Trail from the east. Stay right, heading south. The young forest along the final ascent is dense and permits little sunshine. Soon the return trail from Multnomah Creek Way rejoins the main trail; stay left, continuing southwest, for the top of Larch Mountain.

At 5.7 miles from the trailhead, the Oneonta Trail ends at a bend in the Larch Mountain Road. You are 0.4 mile from the parking lot. Turn right, heading west on the road back to your car.

# LARCH MOUNTAIN LOOP AND SHERRARD POINT

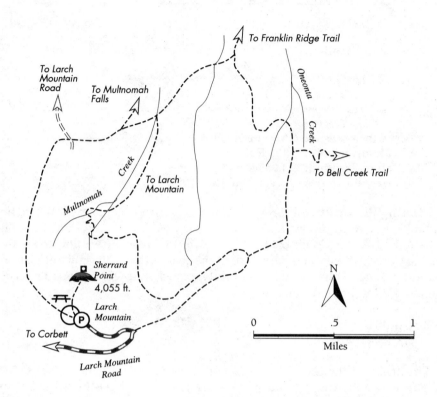

# 11  SHERRARD POINT

See Map on Page 43

| | |
|---|---|
| **General description:** | A very easy walk for a view from the top of Larch Mountain. |
| **Difficulty:** | Easy. |
| **Distance:** | 0.4 mile. |
| **Trail type:** | Well-maintained. |
| **Traffic:** | Heavy. |
| **Best season:** | May to October. |
| **Elevation gain:** | 105 feet. |
| **Maximum elevation:** | 4,055 feet. |
| **Topographic maps:** | Bridal Veil USGS, Bridal Veil Green Trails. |

**Finding the trailhead:** From Portland, take I-84 east just past Troutdale and take Exit 18 for Lewis & Clark State Park. Follow the off–ramp until it ends at the Historic Columbia River Highway and turn left. Follow the main road to Corbett. Two miles past Corbett the road forks; turn right onto Larch Mountain Road. Fourteen miles of pretty, paved, and winding road later is the Larch Mountain Trailhead.

**Key points:**
  0.2  Sherrard Point

**The trail:** At the top of Larch Mountain is Sherrard Point. It is just 0.2 mile from the parking lot, and is the only place you'll get much of a view from the forested peak of Larch Mountain.

The trail to Sherrard Point begins to the right of a large interpretive sign. It is paved most of the way and offers the best view from the top of the mountain.

A few stairs just before the final platform make this lookout inaccessible to wheelchairs. The cement lookout offers interpretive plaques in the direction of each dormant volcano on the horizon. On a clear day it is a special experience to pick out Mounts Jefferson, Hood, St. Helens, Adams, and Rainier. It gives you a big picture of the Gorge area. Sometimes the best views are the easiest to get to.

**General description:** A short day hike underneath Ponytail Falls, with an optional trip to Triple Falls.

**Distance:** 1.8 miles.

**Difficulty:** Easy.

**Traffic:** Heavy.

**Trail type:** Well-maintained.

**Best season:** Year–round depending upon frost line.

**Elevation gain:** 200 feet.

**Maximum elevation:** 300 feet.

**Topographic maps:** Bridal Veil Green Trails and Multnomah Falls USGS.

**Finding the trailhead:** From Portland, take Interstate 84 east to Bridal Veil Exit 28. Follow the off–ramp to the intersection with the Historic Columbia River Highway. Turn left, heading east on Highway 30 for 5.5 miles to the Horsetail Falls Trailhead. Park in the lot on the north side of the road. The Trail 438 is just across the highway, to the left of the Horsetail Falls picnic area. There is ample parking, but no public restrooms.

**Key points:**

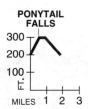

- 0.1   Junction with Gorge Trail 400
- 0.4   Ponytail Falls
- 0.8   Junction with Lookout Spur
- 1.1   Junction with Oneonta Trail 424
- 1.7   Junction with Gorge trail 400
- 1.8   Return to the Historic Columbia River Highway for a 0.5 mile walk back to Horsetail Falls

**The trail:** Horsetail Falls and Ponytail Falls are part of an easy hike with spectacular views, waterfalls, and Oneonta Gorge. You can extend this hike through the Triple Falls option. These features, along with easy accessibility, make for heavy use on weekends. However, this hike is good for hikers of most all ages and abilities.

From the trailhead, gentle switchbacks climb around Horsetail Falls. At 0.1 mile is the intersection with Gorge Trail 400. Stay right, heading south, for Ponytail Falls. Trail 438 continues to climb until it turns west where cliffs block further climbing. It levels out as the trail rounds the bend. At 0.4 mile, Ponytail Falls is on your left. The trail goes right underneath Ponytail Falls, with sheer rock above and the falls crashing down in front of you.

The trail is flat and runs parallel to the highway. Then, at 0.8 mile, turn right, to the north, for a lookout above cliffs several hundred feet high. A marker warns of the dangerous nature of these cliffs, where a 13–year–old boy fell and died near this lookout in 1988. If you do not like heights, stay to the left and skip this lookout.

The main trail turns south and descends into the Oneonta Gorge. Follow a few steep switchbacks down, cross a footbridge, and then climb a few more short switchbacks up the other side of Oneonta Gorge. At 1.1 miles is the intersection with the Oneonta Trail 424. Turn right, heading north, to finish the loop. Left takes you south to Triple Falls.

If you're skipping Triple Falls, after turning right head north for 0.6 mile until you reach the intersection with Gorge Trail 400. Then turn right and head northeast for the last 0.1 mile until you reach the Historic Columbia River Highway.

It is 0.5 mile back along the road to Horsetail Falls. As you follow the road back, be sure to look up the narrow section of Oneonta Gorge. This natural gorge offers wading opportunities. About 1,000 feet up the gorge is 100-foot-high Oneonta Falls. The falls used to be closer to the highway, but as it cut a slit in the basalt, it worked its way upstream, forming a box canyon.

# HORSETAIL AND PONYTAIL FALLS

Also see map on page 48

## TRIPLE FALLS OPTION

It is an extra 1.6 mile round trip to see Triple Falls. If you are wondering why they call it Triple Falls, then turn left at the intersection of the Oneonta Trail 424 and the Horsetail Falls Trail 438. The longer route, Oneonta Gorge Trail to Triple Falls, is mostly level, with one or two steep sections of climbing. Triple Falls has several good lunch spots with views of the falls.

# 13   ONEONTA TRAIL TO LARCH MOUNTAIN

| | |
|---|---|
| **General description:** | An extended point-to-point hike through waterfall-filled Oneonta Gorge to forested Larch Mountain. |
| **Distance:** | 7.7 miles. |
| **Difficulty:** | Difficult. |
| **Traffic:** | Heavy to moderate. |
| **Trail type:** | Well-maintained. |
| **Best season:** | May through October. |
| **Elevation gain:** | 3,840 feet. |
| **Maximum elevation:** | 3,940 feet. |
| **Topographic maps:** | Bridal Veil Green Trails and Multnomah Falls USGS. |

**Finding the trailhead:** From Portland, take Interstate 84 east to Bridal Veil Exit 28. Follow the off-ramp to the intersection with the Historic Columbia River Highway. Turn left, heading east on Highway 30 for 5 miles to a turnoff to the Horsetail Falls Trailhead. The dirt parking area is on the north side of the road and Oneonta Trail 424 starts across the highway to the south.

This trip requires a shuttle vehicle left at Larch Mountain. From Portland, take Interstate 84 east just past Troutdale and take exit 18 for Lewis & Clark State Park. Follow the off-ramp until it ends at the Historic Columbia River Highway and turn left. Follow the main road to Corbett. Two miles past Corbett the road forks; turn right onto Larch Mountain Road. Fourteen miles of pretty, paved, and winding road later is the Larch Mountain Trailhead.

**Key points:**

| | |
|---|---|
| 0.1 | Junction with Gorge Trail 400 |
| 0.7 | Junction with Horsetail Falls Trail 438 |
| 2.7 | Junction with Horsetail Creek Trail 425 |
| 4.6 | Junction with Franklin Ridge Trail 427 |
| 5.1 | Junction with Multnomah spur 446 |
| 5.9 | Junction with Bell Creek Trail 459 |
| 6.8 | Junction with Multnomah Creek Way 444 |
| 7.7 | Larch Mountain Road |

# ONEONTA GORGE

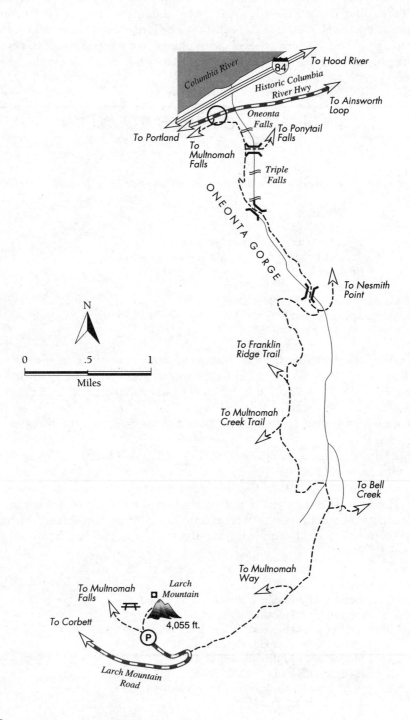

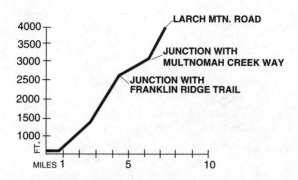

**The trail:** Oneonta Gorge Trail has all of the elements that make for a good overnight trip in the Columbia River Gorge: waterfalls, steep creek-weathered basalt cliffs, and good campsites.

From the trailhead, the trail climbs 0.1 mile to the junction with Gorge Trail 400. Stay left, continuing south and up. The trail is in older fir trees with little sunlight. It rounds a bend into the Oneonta Valley and flattens out until 0.7 mile, the junction with the Trail 438 from Horsetail Falls. Stay right continuing south. The trail climbs two long switchbacks and then runs level again until Triple Falls. Along the way, you can see down into the steep sides of Oneonta Gorge.

At 1.5 miles is Triple Falls. Triple Falls is composed of three spouting 100-foot drops and is an excellent place for lunch. The bridge just past the falls marks the start of a less drastic valley than the one seen up to this point. Oneonta Creek, above the basalt layer, is just a lush Oregon stream. After crossing the bridge there is a possible tent site, but I don't recommend camping here because of the heavy day use.

Past the falls, the trail climbs up the east side of the valley through moss-covered maples and deadfall. The sword ferns add a green touch, while licorice ferns grow out of the moss-covered trunks. The climb is gentle. The trail crosses Oneonta Creek on a bridge and shortly after is a heavily-used campsite at the junction with Horsetail Creek Trail 425 from Nesmith Point. The camp has easy access to water and a good fire ring, but it is not very far off the trail.

Turn right, continuing on Trail 424, for a climb up the west ridge. The elevation gain really picks up here and you should tank up and rest up at the creek before beginning the climb. You might even stay there a night.

At 4.6 miles the trail intersects the Franklin Ridge Trail 427. Only a little sunlight pokes through the dense forest. Stay left for Larch Mountain to the south.

At 5.1 miles is the junction with Multnomah Spur 446. This spot, surrounded by giant firs, is a great place for a nap. After dozing for a bit and drinking some water, turn right, heading southwest, for the climb up Oneonta Trail.

*Oneonta Gorge*

At 6.8 miles into the trip, the Bell Creek Trail 459 joins the Oneonta Trail 424 from the east. Stay right, heading south. The young forest along the final ascent is dense and allows little sunshine to break through. Soon the return trail from Multnomah Creek Way 444 joins the main trail. Stay left, continuing southwest, for the top of Larch Mountain.

At 7.7 miles from the start, the Oneonta Trail ends at a bend in the Larch Mountain Road. You are 0.4 mile from the parking lot. Turn right, heading west on the road, to the summit.

| | |
|---|---|
| **General description:** | A steep, primitive scramble up Rock of Ages Ridge, with views of cliffs and basalt formations galore. |
| **Distance:** | 6 miles. |
| **Difficulty:** | Difficult. |
| **Traffic:** | Light. |
| **Trail type:** | Primitive. |
| **Best season:** | May through October. |
| **Elevation gain:** | 2,940 feet. |
| **Maximum elevation:** | 3,040 feet. |
| **Topographic maps:** | Bridal Veil Green Trails, Multnomah Falls USGS. |

**Finding the Trailhead:** From Portland, take Interstate 84 east to Bridal Veil Exit 28. Follow the off–ramp to the intersection with the Historic Columbia River Highway. Turn left and head east on Highway 30 for 5.5 miles to the Horsetail Falls Trailhead. Park in the lot on the north side of the road. (From Hood River take Exit 35 [Warrendale/Dodson] and drive west on the Columbia Gorge Scenic Highway for 1.5 miles to Horsetail Falls.) Trail 438 is just across the highway to the left of the Horsetail Falls picnic area. There is ample parking, but no public restrooms.

**Key points:**
    0.1   Junction with Gorge Trail 400
    0.3   Unmarked Junction for Rock of Ages Ridge Trail
    0.8   Junction with Lookout Spur
    3.0   Junction with Horsetail Creek Trail 425

**The trail:** The trail up Rock of Ages Ridge is unmaintained, little used and very steep. But it offers breathtaking cliffside views, cool forests, and a good workout. The trail is not as severe as Ruckel Ridge, but it does have a few adrenaline-rush spots. Rock of Ages Ridge is a useful segue to several loop options, either down Nesmith Point Trail or via Horsetail Creek and Oneonta Gorge.

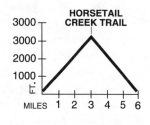

From the trailhead, gentle switchbacks climb around Horsetail Falls. At 0.1 mile is the intersection with Gorge Trail 400. Stay right, heading south, for Ponytail Falls. The trail continues to climb, then turns west where cliffs block further climbing. As the now-level trail rounds the bend, to the left at 0.4 mile is Ponytail Falls. Just as the trail rounds the corner to Ponytail Falls, look up and to the left for the fainter trail. A sign reading "Trail not maintained" is the only marker. Turn left, heading southeast, onto this primitive trail. It heads straight up the slope, splitting and rejoining in several places.

51

# ROCK OF AGES RIDGE

Also see map on page 46

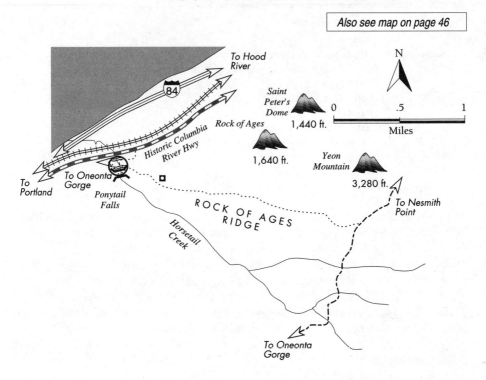

At 0.8 mile is a junction marked only by a cut branch on a fir tree. Straight east is a spur trail to a lookout. At the lookout you need to climb over some rocks to see the sheer cliffs on the other side. This ascent is dangerous. If you want to take a look, be sure to crawl on all fours. On the basalt cliffs you can see an arch-protected cave. Up the ravine you can see a lonely tree in the crevice at the top.

Back down at the cut–branch junction, turn south and continue around and up this steep, primitive trail. The trail climbs for another 0.5 mile before reaching a large rock spine on a ridge covered in moss. Climb to the left around this outcropping to a viewpoint. To the east you can see Beacon Rock, Hamilton Mountain, and Mount St. Helens. Out on the rock spine you can look further east and get a glimpse of Rock of Ages next to Saint Peter's Dome, but it is not a very good angle. The trail continues through the trees up the ridge to the south.

After crossing the rock spine, the trail levels out, then climbs again through the trees. Then, after about 2 miles, the trail levels again. Along the way are cedars and ancient snags from a long–ago fire. Through the trees you'll catch a view of Yeon Mountain. The trail ends at the Horsetail Creek Trail 425 on top of Nesmith/Yeon Plateau. The trail on your right, to the west,

*A hiker enjoys the view from Rock of Ages Ridge.*

takes you to Oneonta Gorge, but is an extra 5.7 miles. The left trail requires a shuttle to John B. Yeon State Park. For description of these sections of trail see the Nesmith/Yeon Loop Hike.

Return to the trailhead via your choice or the same trail. The Rock of Ages trail takes just as long to hike down because of the steep grade.

| | |
|---|---|
| **General description:** | A short 0.4 mile walk through the temperate forest of the Columbia River Gorge. |
| **Distance:** | 0.4 mile. |
| **Difficulty:** | Easy. |
| **Traffic:** | Light. |
| **Trail type:** | Well-maintained. |
| **Best season:** | Year-round. |
| **Elevation gain:** | 40 feet. |
| **Maximum elevation:** | 260 feet. |
| **Topographic maps:** | Bridal Veil Green Trails, Bridal Veil USGS. |

**Finding the trailhead:** From Portland, take Interstate 84 east to Exit 35 for Ainsworth State Park. Follow the off-ramp to the intersection with Columbia River Highway. Turn right, then left, and head west on the Historic Columbia River Highway for 1 mile. The Ainsworth Loop Trailhead is on the south side of the road. Parking and bathrooms are available at the trailhead.

There is also another trailhead 0.1 mile further on the left. The loop can start at either place. However, there are more parking spaces at the first one.

## AINSWORTH LOOP TRAIL

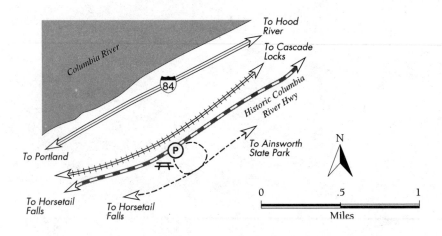

**Key points:**
    0.1   Junction with Gorge Trail 400
    0.2   Junction with Ainsworth Loop Trail
    0.3   Second Ainsworth Trailhead
    0.4   Return to first trailhead

**The trail:** The Ainsworth Loop Trail is not much exercise, but it does provide a relaxing stroll through the forest, away from the crowds at Multnomah Falls. This hike is more interesting if you have a plant field guide along.

From the trailhead, the trail climbs gently for 0.1 mile up to Gorge Trail 400. At the well–marked junction turn right, heading west to another well-marked junction with the Ainsworth Trail. Along the way you can get a feel for the common plants of the Columbia Gorge. Douglas-fir is the most common evergreen. Bigleaf maple is the most common deciduous tree. Bushy vine maple is also common, but it usually grows only to the size of a large bush.

The most noticeable fern is the sword fern, which has a little hitch where the leaves connect to the stem. Oregon grape is also common. It has holly-like leaves and yellow bunches of flowers.

The second junction is also well marked. Turn right again to the second trailhead. From the second trailhead, turn right on a connecting loop trail for the last 0.1 mile to the first trailhead.

# 16   NESMITH POINT AND YEON MOUNTAIN LOOP

| | |
|---|---|
| **General description:** | A long day hike through pristine forests, with incredible views of the Washington Cascades. |
| **Distance:** | 13.1 miles. |
| **Difficulty:** | Difficult. |
| **Traffic:** | Light. |
| **Trail type:** | Maintained. |
| **Best season:** | May through October. |
| **Elevation gain:** | 3,720 feet. |
| **Maximum elevation:** | 3,880 feet. |
| **Topographic maps:** | Bridal Veil and Bonneville Dam Green Trails; Bonneville Dam and Multnomah Falls USGS. |

**Finding the trailhead:** From Portland, take Interstate 84 east to Exit 35 for Warrendale, Dodson. This loop requires a shuttle car left at the Oneonta Gorge Trailhead. From Exit 35 turn right and head west for 2 miles, past Horsetail Falls to the next marked trailhead on your left just past Oneonta Gorge. The Oneonta Trailhead is on the left, and a shaded dirt parking lot is across the road. Leave a car here and drive back on the Historic Columbia River Highway to Exit 35.

At Exit 35, head east on Columbia Gorge Scenic Highway 30 for 2.5 miles to the John B. Yeon State Park Trailhead on the right. There is ample parking, but no public restrooms. Trail 428 to Nesmith Point begins on the west end of the parking lot.

**Key points:**
|       |                                         |
|-------|-----------------------------------------|
| 0.1   | Junction with Trail 400 to Elowah Falls |
| 1.2   | Lookout spur                            |
| 4.6   | Junction with jeep road to Nesmith Point|
| 4.7   | Nesmith Point lookout                   |

**Yeon Mountain Loop:**
|       |                                            |
|-------|--------------------------------------------|
| 4.8   | Return to junction with jeep road          |
| 6.8   | Unmarked junction with old Rock of Ages Ridge Trail |
| 8.1   | Junction with Bell Creek Trail 459         |
| 10.4  | Junction with Oneonta Trail 424            |
| 12.4  | Junction with Horsetail Falls Trail        |
| 13.1  | Oneonta Trailhead                          |

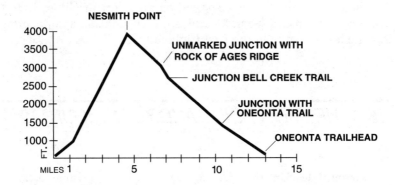

**The trail:** The trail to Nesmith Point and further to Yeon Mountain offers some intense hiking and some incredible views of Mount St. Helens, Mount Adams, and Mount Rainier. From a lookout near Yeon Mountain, you can see all three. Check the weather for a clear forecast. The trail to Nesmith Point can either be a up–and–back hike or a loop, depending upon whether you choose to leave a car at the Oneonta Trailhead. The loop option is longer and involves a ford across Oneonta Creek, but the extra view along the way and the more gradual decent are worth it. I highly recommend the loop option. Either way, this trail is a steep 3,700 foot climb and most of it is in less than 3 miles.

From the trailhead, after a sign at 0.1 mile, is Trail 428 to Nesmith Point. Take the right fork, heading west. The trail continues along a gentle grade for 0.6 mile, through the trees, until a huge landslide is visible on the right. This slide happened during the "Great Flood of '96," as the local media

*Moss-covered slopes along the Nesmith Point Trail.*

billed it. Huge boulders and mounds of dirt surround a few solitary trees that weathered the slide. Luckily the trail turns just before entering the slide. Trail 400, which would have continued west at this point, is no longer there, so there is no junction to speak of. It is scheduled for rebuilding in 1998.

After a mile of long switchbacks is a spur trail, on your left, heading north, to a small lookout. From this lookout is the first of the good views to come. Table and Hamilton mountains are visible across the Gorge. After this short side trip the trail flattens out for a few hundred yards before again climbing steeply on switchbacks.

There are several examples of old–growth fir and cedar as the trail climbs higher. Also, along the way, watch out for Devils club. Devils club has huge leaves much like cow parsnip, but the stems have slivery spikes and emit a chemical that can cause uncomfortable itching and scratching, similar to that caused by nettles. Devils club does, however, bear a very pretty stack of bright red berries late in the season. Look, but don't touch, and definitely don't eat.

When you enter the most shaded and oldest grove of cedars you are close to the end of the steepest climbing. Cresting the ravine makes you appreciate this legitimate power climb. It is 1.5 miles to the top from the crest of the ravine, but it is nothing like the steep ascent before. The trail continues to climb gradually, turning west through younger trees. You get a short glimpse of the McCord Creek valley to the left.

# NESMITH POINT AND YEON MOUNTAIN LOOP

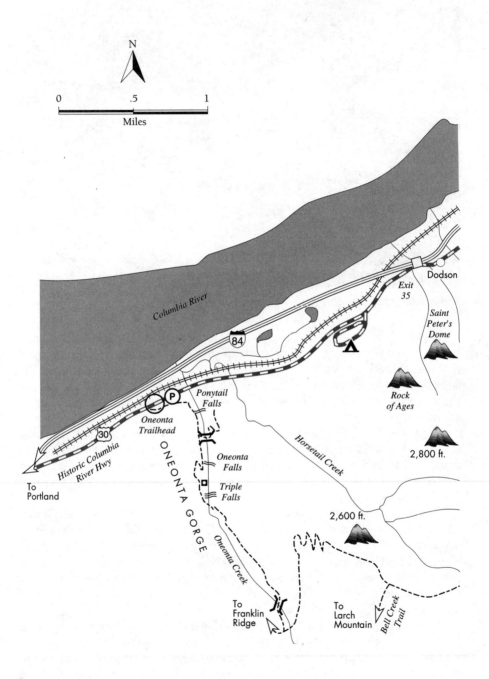

N

0    .5    1
Miles

Columbia River

Dodson

Exit 35

Saint Peter's Dome

84

Rock of Ages

2,800 ft.

Ponytail Falls

Oneonta Trailhead

P

30

Historic Columbia River Hwy

ONEONTA GORGE

Oneonta Falls

Horsetail Creek

Triple Falls

2,600 ft.

To Portland

Oneonta Creek

To Franklin Ridge

To Larch Mountain

Bell Creek Trail

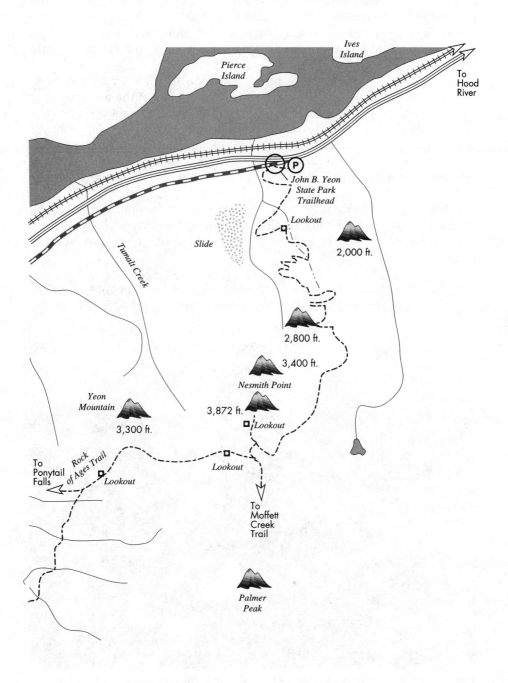

Pierce Island

Ives Island

To Hood River

John B. Yeon State Park Trailhead

P

Lookout

2,000 ft.

Slide

Tumalt Creek

2,800 ft.

3,400 ft.

Nesmith Point

Yeon Mountain

3,300 ft.

3,872 ft.

Lookout

To Ponytail Falls

Rock of Ages Trail

Lookout

Lookout

To Moffett Creek Trail

Palmer Peak

Just before the junction with the old logging road to the top, the trail make a 90 degree right turn to the north. At one point a straight trail connected this trail with the Horsetail Creek Trail 425 to make a loop, but it no longer does. Stay right, heading north, at this unmarked junction. At 4.6 miles is a marked junction with an old logging road to the top of Nesmith Point. Turn right to Nesmith Point.

Congratulations, you have reached the top of a 4.7 mile, 3,720-foot climb. That is an average of 790 feet per mile. However, most of the elevation is in the first 3 miles. The summit is forested, but one spot offers a cliffside view of the Columbia Gorge, Vancouver, and beyond. There is enough room at the top for several parties to find solitude. There is an old abandoned outhouse, not recommended for use, and an old benchmark. Most of the top is protected from the wind and far away from the sounds of the interstate below.

If hiking in the trees makes you hungry for more overlooks, continue on the loop instead of returning via the same route. The Horsetail Creek Trail has several more of these lookouts, similar to the one on top of Nesmith point.

 Doing the loop does involve a tricky ford of Oneonta Creek, so consider this before choosing the loop.

*The 1996 slide that wiped out a section of Gorge trail 400 along the Nesmith Point Trail.*

If continuing on is not an option, because you prefer not to or did not leave a car at the Oneonta Trailhead, the return trip down to the John B. Yeon State Park Trailhead is a steep one. You might want to tighten your laces.

### YEON MOUNTAIN LOOP OPTION

To continue on from the summit, return via the old logging road to the marked junction with Nesmith Point Trail and the old logging road. Turn right, heading west, on the logging road, and less than 0.1 mile farther take another right onto Horsetail Creek Trail 425. The grade descends gradually before levelling off. The surrounding forest is thick and has small diameter trees. When a stand of trees is young there tend to be more trees with smaller diameters. As the forest ages, the weak trees die off, leaving the healthier survivors with more sunlight and less competition. The older a tree gets, the thicker it gets.

At two points the trail passes along the edge of the Yeon Mountain, offering views of the steep Tumalt Creek valley. The first point offers a unique view of the bowl-shaped topography of the valley below. This area is where a major landslide started in 1996 that blocked Interstate 84 completely for several days. Here, you can also see Mount St. Helens, Mount Adams, and Mount Rainier. From the second lookout you get a glimpse of St. Peters Dome, which is a product of layers of Columbia River Basalt weathered away to a pointed solitary formation.

After 6.8 miles and a couple of tremendous views, the trail comes to an unmarked junction with the Rock of Ages Ridge Trail. This trail is not shown on some maps, but the junction is visible on the Multnomah Falls USGS 7.5 minute quadrangle. Stay left, continuing west, at this unmarked junction.

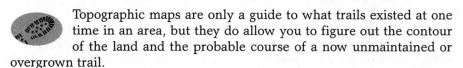 Topographic maps are only a guide to what trails existed at one time in an area, but they do allow you to figure out the contour of the land and the probable course of a now unmaintained or overgrown trail.

At 8.1 miles, is the junction with the Bell Creek Trail 459, which is again not shown on some maps. This junction is marked; stay right, heading west, for Oneonta Trail 424. About 0.5 mile farther, the trail begins a more drastic decent along switchbacks. Soon you can hear the crashing water of Oneonta Creek. The crossing of Oneonta Creek is treacherous, especially early in the summer, when water levels are high. You should make sure you are comfortable crossing a rushing creek like Oneonta before deciding on the loop.

After crossing the creek, turn right, heading north, at the junction with Oneonta Trail 424. There is a well-used campsite at this junction. The trail descends at stream gradient down the gorge, crossing the creek on a log bridge and again on a footbridge before Triple Falls. It is easy to see why Triple Falls got its name from the three shooting tails of water that crash below.

After another mile you'll reach the intersection with the Horsetail Falls Trail 438. Stay left, continuing north, for the Oneonta Trailhead.

# 17   ELOWAH FALLS

|  |  |
|---|---|
| **General description:** | A short day hike to 290-foot-high Elowah Falls. |
| **Distance:** | 1.6 miles. |
| **Difficulty:** | Easy. |
| **Trail type:** | Well-maintained. |
| **Traffic:** | Heavy. |
| **Best season:** | Year-round depending upon frost line. |
| **Elevation gain:** | 100 feet. |
| **Maximum elevation:** | 260 feet. |
| **Topographic maps:** | Bridal Veil and Bonneville Dam Green Trails, Bonneville Dam and Multnomah Falls USGS. |

**Finding the trailhead:** From Portland, take Interstate 84 east to Exit 35 at the Warrendale, Dodson. Turn left, heading east on the Historic Columbia River Highway for 2.5 miles, to the John B. Yeon State Park Trailhead on the right. There is ample parking, but no public restrooms. The trail to Elowah Falls begins on the west end of the parking lot.

**Key points:**
    0.1   Junction with Nesmith Point Trail 428
    0.4   Junction with Upper McCord Creek Falls Trail
    0.8   Bridge below Elowah Falls

**The trail:** Elowah Falls is one of the tallest waterfalls in the Gorge at 290 feet and produces an incredible amount of spray and mist that swirls around the base of the falls. The mist is cold and pure on the skin especially on a hot day. The hike involves a gentle ascent and descent, is short, and does not climb on any ledges, unlike the trail to Upper McCord Creek Falls. This hike is a good hike for people of all ages.

After leaving the trailhead, the trail forks. Take the left fork, heading east, for Elowah Falls. The trail climbs at a gentle grade through middle-aged trees. In the spring watch for trillium, a resident of moist forest floors. Trillium is a flower with three large white petals and three two- to six-inch-long, broadly ovate leaves.

At 0.4 mile is the second junction. The right trail climbs steeply up to Upper McCord Creek Falls. Take the left trail, continuing east for Elowah Falls. Trail 400 drops on switchbacks into the Elowah Glen below the falls. At 0.8 mile is Elowah Falls, crashing down from a height of 290 feet. The

# ELOWAH FALLS AND
# UPPER MCCORD CREEK FALLS

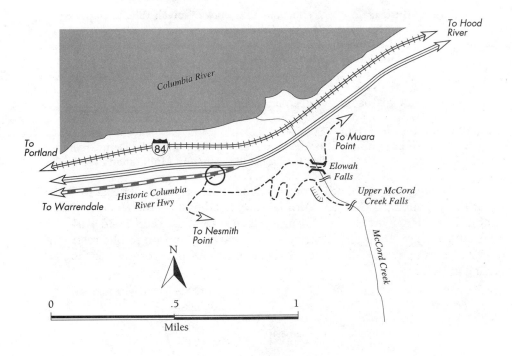

spray from the falls blows across the bridge, especially in spring, making the wood planks slick; watch your footing.

After the bridge, Trail 400 continues, if 0.8 mile wasn't enough. The trail heads to Wahclella Trailhead via Trail 400, passing Munra Point along the way.

From the other side of the bridge you can look up to the cliffs above and see the Upper McCord Creek Trail cut into the face. If the sight of this excites you, try the Upper McCord Creek Trail on the way back.

Return via the same route to the trailhead.

See Map on Page 63

| | |
|---|---|
| **General description:** | A short day hike above Elowah Falls to Upper McCord Creek Falls. |
| **Distance:** | 2.2 miles. |
| **Difficulty:** | Moderate. |
| **Traffic:** | Moderate. |
| **Trail type:** | Maintained. |
| **Best season:** | Year–round, depending upon frost line. |
| **Elevation gain:** | 380 feet. |
| **Maximum elevation:** | 560 feet. |
| **Topographic maps:** | Bridal Veil Green Trails, Bonneville Dam Green Trails, Bonneville Dam and Multnomah Falls USGS. |

**Finding the trailhead:** From Portland, take Interstate 84 east to Exit 37 at the Warrendale, Dodson. Turn left and head east on the Historic Columbia River Highway 30 for 2.5 miles to the John B. Yeon State Park. The trailhead is on the right. There is ample parking, but no public restrooms. The trail to Upper McCord Creek Falls begins on the west end of the parking lot.

**Key points:**
0.1  Junction with Nesmith Point Trail
0.4  Junction with Gorge Trail 400 to Elowah Falls
1.1  Upper McCord Creek Falls

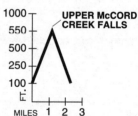

**The trail:** If you liked the view of Elowah Falls and want to see more of it, this is the trail for you. The path takes you along a sheer rock face to Upper McCord Creek Falls. The trail climbs almost 400 feet of switchbacks; the path along the cliff has a guardrail, but looking down can still give you the shivers.

  Don't do this hike if heights scare you.

After leaving the trailhead, the trail forks. Take the left fork on Trail 400 and head east for Upper McCord Creek Falls. The trail climbs at a gentle grade, with Douglas-fir and Oregon grape below.

At 0.4 mile is the second junction. The left trail is to Elowah Falls. Take the right fork, heading south, and begin the climb to Upper McCord Creek Falls. The trail takes one vary long switchback past several large, rusted water pipes. Plants and water are vigorously decaying these old pieces of metal, proving that even old metal pipes are biodegradable.

After the rusted water pipes, the trail traverses the ridge toward McCord Creek. The trail flattens out as you begin to walk on the face of a cliff. The steel railing on the left offers reassurance to the hiker, but in one spot the railing is missing. There is plenty of room to safely hike this trail, but if you're prone to vertigo, I don't suggest it.

The view below is a new perspective on the 290 feet of waterfall. The impact of the water on the rock cuts and shapes the landscape below.

After leaving the guardrail, the trail comes to Upper McCord Creek Falls, which is less exhilarating than the hike to it. The less than 100-foot falls is hard to appreciate as much as Elowah Falls. If it was in an area without as many spectacular waterfalls as the Gorge, it might get more recognition.

Return to the trailhead via the same route.

## 19   MUNRA POINT

| | |
|---:|:---|
| **General description:** | A steep scramble of a day hike up Munra Point on a primitive trail. |
| **Distance:** | 5.2 miles |
| **Difficulty:** | Difficult. |
| **Traffic:** | Light. |
| **Trail type:** | Unmaintained. |
| **Best season:** | May through October. |
| **Elevation gain:** | 1,500 feet. |
| **Maximum elevation:** | 1,600 feet. |
| **Topographic maps:** | Bonneville Dam Green Trails (trail does not appear on USGS or Trails of the Columbia Gorge). |

**Finding the trailhead:** From Portland, take Interstate 84 east to Exit 40 at the Bonneville Fish Hatchery. Turn right, then right again, heading south towards the Wahclella Falls Trailhead. Follow the right loop around to find ample parking, but no public restrooms. The trail to Munra Point begins on Gorge Trail 400 heading west. It starts on the old scenic highway on the west side of the road just as you enter the trailhead drive. If the Wahclella Falls/Tanner Creek Trailhead has recently been washed out by ice storms and is not accessible, you can start at John B. Yeon State Park instead (see the Elowah Falls Hike).

**Key points:**
- 0.2   Junction with jeep road
- 1.4   Junction to Munra Point Trail
- 2.6   Junction with lookout spur

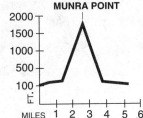

MUNRA POINT

**The trail:** The hike up Munra Point is short, steep, and often treacherous if you are not used to steep ascents without many switchbacks. The trail does not take you all the way up, but the views are nice and the trail is one of the least used in the area.

From the trailhead, Trail 400 crosses Tanner Creek immediately on an old bridge of the Historic Columbia River Highway. Then the trail veers left and uphill at a marked junction. At the end of a switchback the trail was washed out. It is still passable enough to cut up to the next switch. This is one place where it is acceptable to cut.

At 0.2 mile, stay right as an old road forks steeply left. The road ends up at the powerlines above. The right fork continues on Trail 400 parallel to Interstate 84 with plentiful Himalayan blackberries along the way.

At 1.4 mile, just before dropping into Moffet Creek, an unmarked trail forks to the left. Take it, and head south on Munra Point Trail. This trail is not maintained and less used than most, but it is not hard to spot. If you cross Moffet Creek, you've gone too far.

After the junction, the trail climbs through a mixed forest of fir and oak trees along switchbacks, and then straight up. The path splits and veers around trees as you scramble up. When you have to choose between a left or right fork, go right for an easier path up. This primitive trail is almost vertical and often requires going on all fours.

*Hamilton Mountain from Munra Point.*

# MUNRA POINT

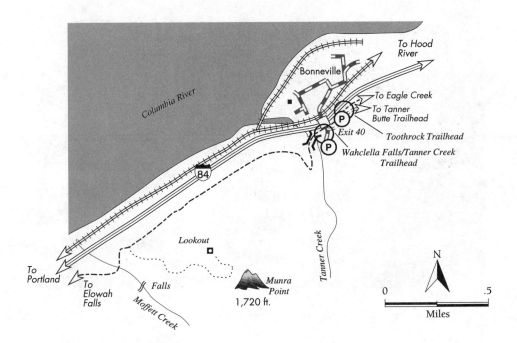

To Hood River

Bonneville

Columbia River

To Eagle Creek

To Tanner Butte Trailhead

Exit 40

Toothrock Trailhead

Wahclella Falls/Tanner Creek Trailhead

84

Lookout

Tanner Creek

To Portland

To Elowah Falls

Falls

Moffett Creek

Munra Point

1,720 ft.

N

0                    .5

Miles

 When scrambling up a steep slope, use stable trees like the railing on a staircase to pull yourself up.

Just before the top the trail forks, and the right fork continues up the ridge over steep rock climbs. The left trail takes you out onto a lookout. This gives you a nice tunnel view down the Gorge and a view of Table Mountain and Hamilton Mountain on the other side.

On the way back, to get away from the sounds of Interstate 84, turn left at the unmarked junction and drop down to a trail leading to a ford across Moffet Creek. The rushing water drowns out the sounds of the outside world and offers a soothing rest spot after your adventurous climb.

Return via Trail 400 to get back to the Wahclella Falls Trailhead.

## TANNER CREEK AREA OVERVIEW:

All trails in this area start from a single trailhead at the old Wahclella Falls/Tanner Creek Trailhead. The access road, FS 777, will remain closed to vehicles for the 5.1 miles to the Tanner Creek Trail and the 2.1 miles to the Tanner Butte Trailhead, extending both of those trips considerably. The road

*Moffet Creek.*

is mountain-bike-accessible in addition to being a pleasant walk. Also from Exit 40, you can find a new mult-use path, constructed in 1996 between the Wahclella Falls/Tanner Creek trailhead and the Eagle Creek Area. It is paved and open to everything from in-line skates to mountain bikes, although there is one section of stairs that could make wheeled progress difficult. Despite the ice flood that washed out most of the trailhead in 1997, this is still the place to start Wahclella Falls, Tanner Creek, and Tanner Butte hikes.

Note: Since this writing, anew trailhead, the Toothrock Trailhead, has been opened, 0.7 mile down FS 777, on the left. It offers parking for all three of the aformentioned hikes and access to the multiuse path.

| | |
|---:|:---|
| **General description:** | A gradual hike to spectacular Wahclella Falls. |
| **Distance:** | 1.8 miles. |
| **Difficulty:** | Easy. |
| **Traffic:** | Heavy. |
| **Trail type:** | Well-maintained. |
| **Best season:** | Year–round, depending upon frost line. |
| **Elevation gain:** | 260 feet. |
| **Maximum elevation:** | 360 feet. |
| **Topographic maps:** | Trails of the Columbia Gorge Map or Bonneville Dam Green Trails (trail does not appear on USGS). |

**Finding the trailhead:** From Portland, take Interstate 84 east to Exit 40 at the Bonneville Fish Hatchery. Turn right and right again, heading south to the Wahclella Falls Trailhead. Follow the right loop around to find ample parking, but no public restrooms. Trail 436 to Wahclella Falls begins on the far end of the loop on an old road. (This trailhead was severely damaged by ice storms in 1997, and you may have to park at the new Toothrock Trailhead just up the road toward Tanner Butte Trail.)

*Cascade along the Wahclella Falls Trail.*

# WAHCLELLA FALLS

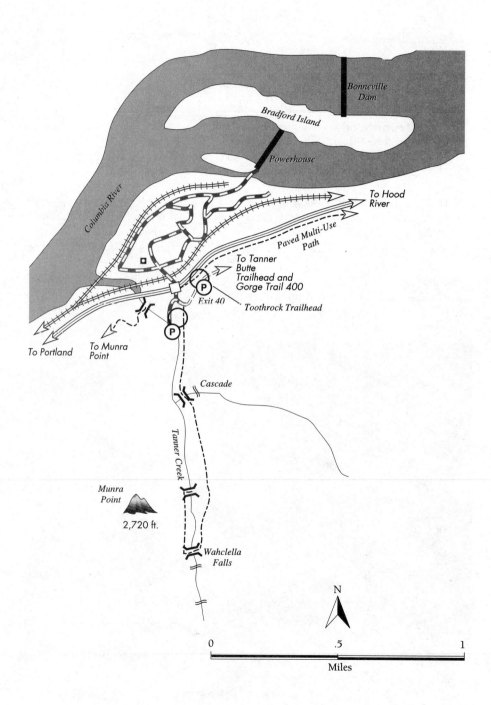

Bonneville
Dam

Bradford Island

Powerhouse

Columbia River

To Hood
River

Paved Multi-Use
Path

To Tanner
Butte
Trailhead and
Gorge Trail 400

P

Exit 40

Toothrock Trailhead

P

To Portland

To Munra
Point

Cascade

Tanner Creek

Munra
Point

2,720 ft.

Wahclella
Falls

N

| 0 | | .5 | | 1 |
Miles

**Key points:**

0.7   Junction with top loop.
0.9   Wahclella Falls.

**The trail:** Wahclella Falls Trail 436 is very pretty and flat. It showcases one of the Columbia River Gorge's most memorable waterfalls. This hike does not have any scary ledges for those who don't like heights, and it is a good hike for children. The trailhead took a major hit during the ice floods of 1997 but it should be rebuilt by 1998.

From the trailhead, Wahclella Falls Trail 436 travels 0.3 mile on an old road next to Tanner Creek. It then crosses a short bridge. A cascade of water is on the left. The trail continues along Tanner Creek until 0.7 mile, where the trail forks. Both forks lead to Wahclella Falls, but the right fork is slightly more gentle. This description follows the left fork, continuing south.

The left fork climbs up for a bit before dropping through a grove of cedars to Wahclella Falls. Here you'll get a good up-front view of the falls and the narrow shoot of water above it. Then the trail crosses the creek next to shiny, water-beaten logs. Next you pass a small cave underneath the perspiring rock. The loop follows the creek downstream before crossing another bridge to rejoin the main trail.  Follow the main trail downstream to the trailhead.

   On hot days, waterfalls are the coolest places to hike.

---

# 21   TANNER CREEK TRAIL

| | |
|---|---|
| **General description:** | A short day hike, inaccessible except by foot or mountain bike. |
| **Distance:** | 5.1 miles in on an old access road, plus a 2.5-mile round-trip hike. |
| **Difficulty:** | Moderate. |
| **Traffic:** | Light. |
| **Trail type:** | Maintained. |
| **Best season:** | Year-round, depending on frost line. |
| **Elevation gain:** | 50 feet. |
| **Maximum elevation:** | 1,360 feet. |
| **Topographic maps:** | Bonneville Dam Green Trails and Tanner Butte USGS. |

**Finding the trailhead:** From Portland, take Interstate 84 east to Exit 40 for the Bonneville Fish Hatchery. Turn right and then left, heading east, up Forest Road 777. Turn left after 0.1 mile and park in the Toothrock Trailhead Trail 431 starts just before the end of the road, on the south side. The road

# TANNER CREEK

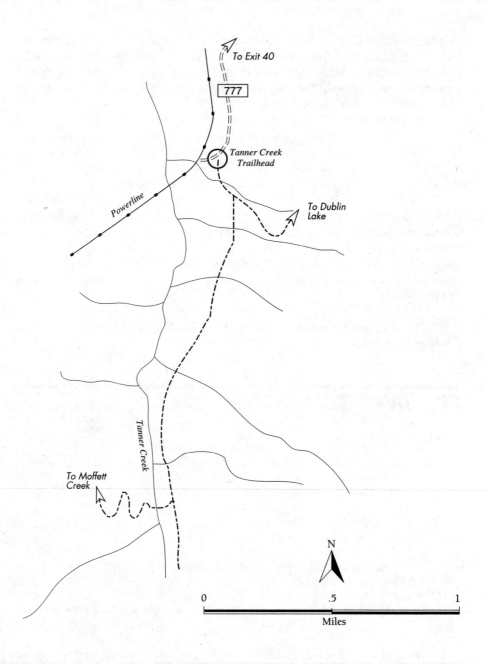

To Exit 40

777

Tanner Creek
Trailhead

Powerline

To Dublin
Lake

Tanner Creek

To Moffett
Creek

N

0          .5          1
Miles

was washed out in 1996 and was not yet reconstructed as of this writing. The Forest Service says that the road will reopen, because Bonneville Power needs access to its towers. Even then it is unlikely to provide vehicle access. Until it is reopened it makes a great mountain bike ride or extended walk of 5.1 miles to reach the Tanner Creek Trailhead.

### Key points:
    0.5   Tanner Cutoff Trail 448
    1.0   Moffet Creek Trail 430
    1.25  End of trail, Campsite

**The trail:** Tanner Creek Trail 431 is not as scenic as the road to it, but it offers relatively secluded camping opportunities after just a short walk. The road to the trailhead may not be open. If the road in is not open or is closed to motorized use, it offers more views of the valley then the trail ahead for hikers and mountain bikers. I suggest mountain biking to the trailhead and then hiking the rest of the way.

From the trailhead, pass two trailhead signs. The trail goes through young, mostly deciduous forest with lush vegetation. It crosses several streams at a level grade.

At 0.5 mile is the marked junction with the Tanner Cutoff Trail. This trail does not receive heavy use and may be difficult to follow up to the Tanner Butte Trail 401. Tanner Butte Trail 401 is more easily accessed, back a couple

*Tanner Creek at the Moffet Creek Trail ford.*

of miles on the access road. (See Tanner Butte Hike).

At 1 mile you reach the junction with Moffet Creek Trail 431. Moffet Creek Trail 431 forks right, heading west. It is hard to ford Tanner Creek in the spring, in order to access the Moffet Creek Trail. The trail on the other side is not a well-used trail, but it is followable with good route-finding skills. Stay left, continuing south on the Tanner Creek Trail 430.

At 1.25 miles, Tanner Creek Trail 430 peters out. There is a small campsite with 1-2 tent sites, a fire ring, and easy water access. A large, burned root nearby hints at the fiery past of this area. Stay the night or return to your car via the access road.

---

## 22    TANNER BUTTE

| | |
|---|---|
| **General description:** | A strenuous, waterless climb to Tanner Butte and Dublin Lake. |
| **Distance:** | 16.6 miles. |
| **Difficulty:** | Difficult. |
| **Traffic:** | Moderate. |
| **Trail type:** | Maintained. |
| **Best season:** | May through October. |
| **Elevation change:** | 3,400 feet. |
| **Maximum elevation:** | 4,500 feet. |
| **Topographic maps:** | Bonneville Dam Green Trails and Tanner Butte USGS. |

**Finding the trailhead:** From Portland, take Interstate 84 east to Exit 40 for the Bonneville Fish Hatchery. Turn right, and then left, up Forest Road 777—turn left after 0.1 mile and park at Toothrock Trailhead. It is another 2.1 miles to the Tanner Butte Trail 401, just before the road crosses a creek.

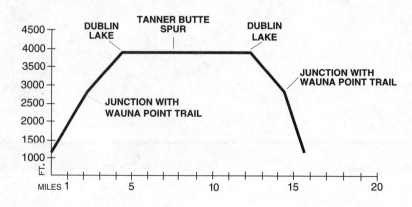

*The ghost-like evidence of a past forest along the Tanner Creek Trail.*

The road was washed out in 1996 and may not be open. Until it is reopened, the walk will be slightly extended.

**Key points:**
| | |
|---|---|
| 2.2 | Junction with Wauna Point Trail (Unmaintained) |
| 4.3 | Junction with Tanner Cutoff Trail 448 |
| 4.4 | Junction with Dublin Lake Spur |
| 7.8 | Junction with Scramble Route up Tanner Butte |
| 8.3 | Tanner Butte |

**The trail:** Tanner Butte is not the easiest hike in the Gorge and there is not much water along the trail. It does, however, go to one of the most prominent high points on the Oregon side of the Gorge, and offers some spectacular views. The best way to do this hike is to make a two-night stay at Dublin Lake with a day trip to the top of Tanner Butte. If you want to go farther, the next good camping spot is Big Cedar Springs on the Eagle Tanner Trail 433. I do not recommend staying at Tanner Springs, especially late in the season when there might not be any water there. Besides, it is one of the least pleasant camping spots I came across in the Gorge.

Begin at the Tanner Butte Trailhead or however far up Tanner Road you made it. Tanner Butte Trailhead is well marked, and the trail leaves the road just before crossing a rushing creek; this is a good place to filter water if you didn't pack enough. The next water source is Dublin Lake. The trail climbs steeply on switchbacks, with virtually no views.

At 2.2 miles you reach the junction with an old trail to Wauna Point (not to be confused with the Wauna Viewpoint Trail from Eagle Creek). This unmaintained trail receives quite a few curious hikers and is well worn. It dead-ends in the trees at a sign reading "Wauna Point." The only view is of a tree-carved smiley face, because the joke is on you. This is not actually Wauna Point. To actually reach Wauna Point, you would have to scramble down another 0.25 mile and out onto a treacherous ledge. I don't recommend this side trip—it could scare the daylights out of you. At the junction with the unmaintained trail to Wauna Point, there is a campsite. It has room for 2-3 tents and a nice fire ring, but there is no water.

To continue toward Tanner Butte, turn right and head south on the Tanner Butte Trail 401. The trail is pretty much level up to the junction with Tanner Cutoff Trail 448. This trail receives light use and is hard to follow. Continue straight, heading south for another 0.1 mile to the junction with Dublin Lake Trail.

At 4.4 miles, turn left heading east for Dublin Lake. Even if you do not want to camp at Dublin Lake it is necessary to stop for water. Dublin Lake is a small pond that supports a healthy population of brook trout and salamanders, which, when swimming along the bottom of the sunlit lake can look like brook trout. They aren't as tasty, though.

At Dublin Lake there is not a lot of room for tents—but maybe you'll find one spot that works. If someone already has that spot, it could be hard to find a place to pitch a tent.

# TANNER BUTTE

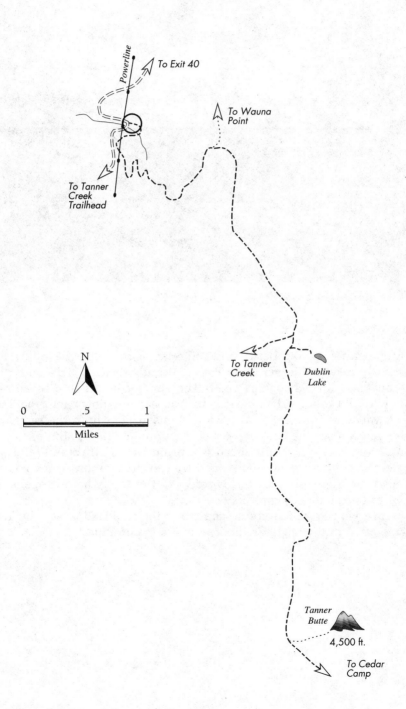

*Tanner Butte from Ruckel Creek Trail.*

After setting up your base camp and relaxing for the night, return to the main trail. Take the Tanner Butte Trail 401 south; the trail is flat and eventually becomes an old logging road. The canopy opens into meadows of beargrass and other subalpine plants. You can see down into the Tanner Creek valley to the west, and towards Benson Plateau to the east. To the south you can see the half tree–covered summit of Tanner Butte.

At 7.8 miles from the trailhead is a primitive cutoff route to the top of Tanner. Since there is no maintained trail to the summit, work your way through the dense spruce and fir forest to the top, where it opens up to views of the surrounding peaks.

Return via the same route to camp and the trailhead or see the Tanner Loop Option in the Eagle Creek description to continue.

# EAGLE CREEK
# RECREATION AREA

## Overview:

The Eagle Creek Campground dates back to 1916, when it was one of the first public recreation sites in Oregon. You can still visit the Civilian Conservation Corps–era style log buildings at the picnic area. Eagle Creek, second only to Multnomah Falls in popularity, is the trail with the most most waterfalls of any hike in the Gorge and offers day, overnight, and extended trip options. You can see three waterfalls in a day trip to Tunnel Falls. You can spend a night at Tenas Camp and hike out. You can shuttle a car to Whatum Lake. Or you can do a two- to three- to four-day loop via Tanner Butte. This description covers the entire route, but you can cut it short at any time. My favorite spot, however was the Big Cedar Camp. It is hard to reach, but the old-growth cedar was the best in the Gorge.

Note that in 1997, ice floods took out the suspension bridge over Eagle Creek to Wauna Viewpoint and the Tanner Butte Loop. But you can make use of the new multi-use trail between Eagle Creek and Tanner Creek to complete the loop and access Wauna Viewpoint. The bridge is scheduled to be reconstructed by 1998.

### SPECIAL REGULATIONS

1. No fires in the Eagle Creek Corridor.
2. No fires outside of designated campsites or within 200 feet of Whatum Lake.
3. No camping outside of designated sites or within 200 feet of Whatum Lake

| | |
|---|---|
| **General description:** | The second most famous and perhaps most enjoyable hike in the Gorge. |
| **Distance:** | 13.3 miles. |
| **Difficulty:** | Easy to Punch Bowl Falls, difficult to Whatum Lake and Tanner Butte Loop. |
| **Traffic:** | Heavy. |
| **Trail type:** | Well–maintained. |
| **Best season:** | May to October. |
| **Elevation gain:** | 3,800 feet to Whatum Lake. |
| **Maximum elevation:** | 3,960 feet. |
| **Topographic maps:** | Trails of the Columbia Gorge or Bonneville Dam, Tanner Butte and Whatum Lake USGS or Bonneville Dam Green Trails. |

**Finding the trailhead:** From Portland, take Interstate 84 east to Exit 41, which is accessible only from the eastbound side. Turn right, heading south past the fish hatchery, and stay along the creek for 0.3 mile to the Eagle Creek Trailhead.

To do the trip one–way to Whatum Lake, you must leave a vehicle at Whatum Lake. To get there, drive east to Hood River Exit 62, turn right, and follow the signs toward the city center on Oak. Turn right at the 13th Street stoplight and head south. Follow the main route. Stay left on Tucker Road, following the signs to Dee after bending left and right. At Dee, turn right on Lost Lake Road, cross railroad tracks, and stay left at the fork. Follow the well–marked paved Forest Road 1310 for 10 miles to the Whatum Lake Trailhead, which is on your right.

**Key points:**
- 1.5    Metlako Falls
- 2.1    Punch Bowl
- 3.3    High Bridge
- 3.7    Tenas Camp
- 4.7    Wy'East Camp
- 5.0    Eagle Benson Trail 434
- 5.3    Blue Grouse Camp
- 6.0    Tunnel Falls
- 7.6    Junction with Eagle-Tanner Trail 433
- 9.8    Junction with Indian Springs Trail 435
- 13.3    Whatum Lake Campsite and Trailhead

**The Trail:** Eagle Creek Trail 440 is second only to Multnomah Falls in popularity, being the hike with more waterfalls than any other in the Columbia Gorge. It is also one of the most flexible, offering day, overnight, and extended backpacking options.

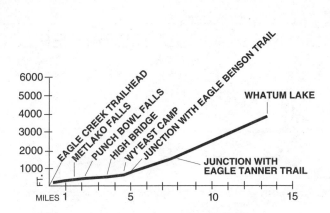

The path is well–beaten and wide as it follows rushing Eagle Creek. The first stretch is a little cliffy and one spot has a 20–foot drop. There is a cable handrail to steady your stride. The trail is flat and high above Eagle Creek.

At 1.5 miles look for a spur trail on your right for a view of Metlako Falls. If you think Metlako Falls is spectacular, you are in for a good day, because the best are yet to come.

At 1.8 miles is the lower Punch Bowl Overlook Trail—this gives you a view of Punch Bowl from a distance. At 2.1 miles you reach the Punch Bowl Overlook. A guardrail prevents hikers from scrambling below, but you can still get a good picture from the lookout.

The Punch Bowl Falls is definitely not a spectacular falls, but the size of the deep pool or "bowl" makes it a spectacular scene, like a fountain in a lake. This is probably why the name emphasizes water punching into a bowl rather than the actual fall.

The trail continues on a level grade. The High Bridge, at 3.3 miles, crosses Eagle Creek on a steel bridge above a narrow gorge much like Oneonta Gorge. The trail is cliffy, but again there is protective cable along the way.

At 3.5 miles, shortly after High Bridge is the first camp on your right. It has 2-3 tent sites, but no easy access to water. There is another camp at 3.6 miles with 1-2 tent sights, but again there is no water access.

At 3.7 miles is the Tenas Camp, with multiple tent sites and an outhouse, old fire rings, and water access. Tenas Camp receives heavy use and is probably not your best option for privacy. There isn't much of a view, either.

About 0.3 mile after crossing the next bridge is another camp. It is near water and has room for 3-4 tent sites.

This area burned in 1902, and along the trail is mostly regrown Douglas–fir and a covering of vine maple. Before reaching Wy'East Camp you'll pass another camp near water with 2-3 tent sites. Then cross Wy'East Creek, which dries up in late September. Wy'East Camp is equipped with multiple tent sites right next to Eagle Creek. Water is easy to get. Fires are not permitted, though camp stoves are.

At 5.2 miles is the junction with Eagle Benson Trail 434. The trail receives moderate use, but the junction is marked.

Next is the Blue Grouse Camp, which has several tent sites and easy

# EAGLE CREEK AND EAGLE TANNER LOOP

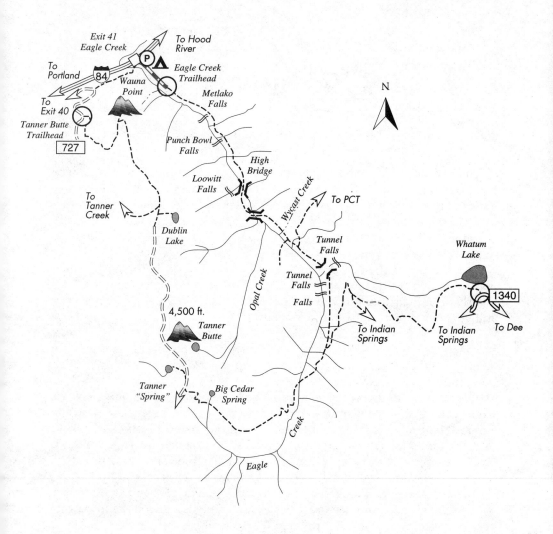

water access. It is a slightly more private setting than Wy'East Camp. The farther you get from the trailhead, the fewer people.

At 6 miles is Tunnel Falls. The tunnel underneath the falls makes the name obvious, but it isn't a dry tunnel. The sweating rock and spray will wet your forehead if you don't wear a hat.

After Tunnel Falls, there is another falls on the main river and a camp just above it. There are several tent sites, and water is available if you go a second falls further. It is remarkably scenic.

After 7 miles is the "7.5 mile camp" by the stream. It has 3-4 tent sites,

*Punch Bowl Falls from the lower lookout along the Eagle Creek Trail.*

fire rings, and easy water access. You'll reach it just before crossing two streams. The trail here is in an old burn area with huge snags and dense foliage.

At 7.6 miles is the junction with the Eagle Tanner Trail 433, which does not receive the heavy use that the path to Whatum Lake does. Turn left, heading east, on the Eagle Creek Trail. There is one fantastic lookout along the way that gives you a view of the Eagle Creek Valley.

At 9.8 miles is the junction with Trail 435 to Indian Springs. Stay left, heading east. There is one campsite on this last stretch, but you might want to wait for Whatum Lake. At Whatum Lake there are several nice campsites on the south shore of the lake, and the lake had brook trout when I fished it.

---

### TANNER BUTTE LOOP OPTION:

Instead of turning left (north) at 7.6 mile junction with the Eagle-Tanner Trail 433, turn right (south). The path is less used because most travelers make the point-to-point hike to Whatum Lake, but here is a chance to go deep in the heart of the Mark O. Hatfield (Columbia) Wilderness.

The trail is relatively flat, with some gradual climbing, until at 8.5 miles the trail crosses the West Fork of Eagle Creek. There is a camp just before the crossing in dense alder and maple forest. The ford is tough in spring. There is room for only 1-2 tent sites and easy water access.

After the ford, the trail is overgrown with sword ferns vine maple and devils club. There are many small-diameter fallen trees, which indicate light use. Don't plan on this section to be cleared: because of its remoteness it is not a top maintenance priority.

The trail climbs more steeply, passing through some very dense, young forest. The canopy is so thick that is some places the forest floor cannot support shrubs. At 11.5 miles (3.9 miles after leaving the main Eagle Creek Trail) is Big Cedar Spring Camp. The camp rests amongst some excellent old growth trees, the biggest I saw in the Gorge, some 500-year-old cedar and fir. These are especially pretty after the dense forest on the trip in. The spring ensures water even in September, and there is room for only one tent.

The next section of trail is a nightmare for a trail crew. This remote section climbs on switchbacks, with huge six foot diameter trees across the trail. It requires some route finding skills, but mostly just finding the trail on the other side of massive blowdowns.

After the short climb, the trail goes past a pond. This muddy water is a better bet than counting on the supposed Tanner "Spring" camp appearing on some maps.

After 13.1 miles (5.0 miles after leaving the main Eagle Creek Trail) is the junction with Tanner Butte Trail 401, which is an old logging road. Turn right, heading north.

At 13.4 miles, the junction with Tanner "Spring" spur trail is marked. Turn left, heading west, to a campsite with 1-2 sites. Don't count on water here; if there is water early in the season, it is a 0.25 mile walk west. There

*The Punch Bowl.*

is no view either.

Past the spur to the "spring" camp is a marked junction with an unmaintained ascent of Tanner Butte. A scramble route works its way through the dense spruce and fir forest to the top. It opens up to views of the surrounding area, and you can cut back down (north) to the trail.

At 17.3 miles into the trip is the junction with a marked trail to Dublin Lake. It supports brook trout and has room for 1-2 tents, but the camp is right on lake.

Next about 0.2 miles further is Tanner Cutoff Trail 448, which offers access to the lightly used Tanner Creek Trail (See Tanner Creek Hike).

At the border of the wilderness area a trail to Wauna Point splits right. It is a scary thing to climb all the way out onto Wauna Point and I wouldn't recommend it. It is no shortcut to Eagle Creek. At this junction there is a campsite with room for 2-3 tent sites and no water. Stay left heading northwest.

The rest of the descent to FS 777 is steep, with switchbacks and no water. Once on the road, turn right heading east along the road. Ordinarily, you could cut over on Gorge Trail 400 from this point back to Eagle Creek Trailhead, but because the suspension bridge may still be out, you might have to use the multi-use path connecting Eagle Creek and Tanner Creek/Wahclella Falls Trailhead.

| General description: | A short, but uphill, climb to a lookout beneath the powerlines. |
|---|---|
| Distance: | 3.6 miles. |
| Difficulty: | Moderate. |
| Traffic: | Usually heavy, but could be pretty light until the suspension bridge is fixed. |
| Trail type: | Well-maintained. |
| Best season: | Year-round, depending upon frost line. |
| Elevation gain: | 1,100 feet. |
| Maximum elevation: | 1,200 feet. |
| Topographic maps: | Bonneville Dam Green Trails and Bonneville Dam USGS. |

**Finding the trailhead:** From Portland, take Interstate 84 east to Eagle Creek Recreation Area Exit 41, which is accessible only from the eastbound side. Turn right, heading south, and drive past the fish hatchery along the creek for 0.1 mile. Before reaching the visible suspension bridge over Eagle Creek, park on the left by the picnic area. Bathrooms are available back toward the hatchery or 0.2 mile further at the Eagle Creek Trailhead. The trail starts across the suspension bridge. (Note: The suspension bridge was washed out in 1997, and you may have to start from Toothrock Trailhead. See Tanner Butte)

**Key points:**
    0.1    Junction with Shady Glen Interpretive Trail
    0.9    Junction with Gorge Trail 400
    1.8    Wauna Viewpoint

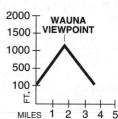

**The trail:** Wauna Viewpoint is a common-sense alternative to actually ascending Wauna Point. It has one major drawback: the powerlines. There's no getting around it, the view is just not as pretty with the powerlines. This trail is similar to the one to Buck Point on the Ruckel Ridge Trail, but offers a slightly better view of Bonneville Dam and Table Mountain.

Trail 402 starts across the bridge. After crossing, you reach a junction with the Shady Glenn Interpretive Trail, one of the by-products of increased hiker participation in the outdoors. Stay right, heading west. The trail climbs along the side of the Eagle Creek valley toward the Columbia. Large firs and plenty of sunlight add to the trail's atmosphere.

At 0.9 mile is a well-marked junction with Gorge Trail 400, which is straight ahead. Turn left, heading south up the hill. The trail climbs on

# WAUNA VIEWPOINT

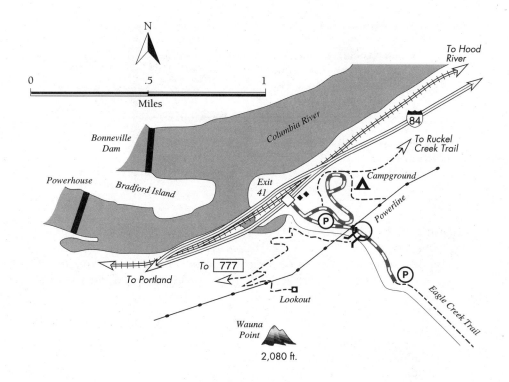

switchbacks until the only cover is several large towers. BPA towers do mean that there are no trees and no trees makes for a better view. You can see across to Table Mountain and the peaks of the Washington Cascades.

Return via the same route to the trailhead.

| | |
|---|---|
| **General Description:** | An adventurous day hike atop a rocky cliff–sided ridge into the Mark O. Hatfield Wilderness. |
| **Distance:** | 8 miles. |
| **Difficulty:** | Difficult. |
| **Traffic:** | Moderate. |
| **Trail type:** | Primitive hiker trail up Ruckel Ridge, well-maintained down Ruckel Creek. |
| **Best season:** | May through October. |
| **Elevation gain:** | 3,650 feet. |
| **Maximum elevation:** | 3,750 feet. |
| **Topographic maps:** | Bonneville Dam Green Trails, Bonneville Dam, Carson USGS. |

**Finding the trailhead:** From Portland, take Interstate 84 east to Exit 41 at the Eagle Creek Recreation Area. Follow the off–ramp. Turn right, then left, and park at the lot in front of the restrooms. Do not try to drive up to the campground. The trailhead is 200 yards up the campground road on your left.

### Key points:
    0.75   End Buck Point Trail 439
    3.3    Junction with Ruckel Creek Trail
    3.7    Junction with trail 405D
    7.6    Junction with Gorge Trail 400
    8.0    Campground Junction with Buck Point Trail 439

**The trail:**  The Ruckel Ridge Trail is not for people who are scared of heights, out of shape, or without sturdy footwear. The primitive trail climbs up steep rock tallus slopes and is on top of a narrow ridge, and at one point the trail crosses a section of ridge only 4 feet wide. The experience is exhilarating, but also dangerous if taken lightly. If you want to avoid the ridge, a steep hike up the Ruckel Creek Trail is a good option, but not as scenic.

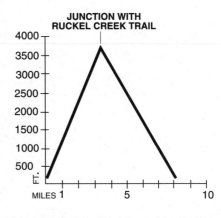

From the parking lot, walk up the campground road for about 200 yards to the trailhead marker on the left side of the road. Follow this trail around the campground to the intersection with Gorge Trail 400 at 0.1 mile and take

# RUCKEL RIDGE LOOP

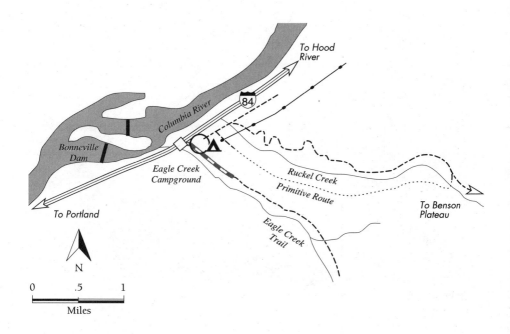

To Hood River

Columbia River

84

To Portland

Bonneville Dam

Eagle Creek Campground

Ruckel Creek Primitive Route

Eagle Creek Trail

To Benson Plateau

N

0    .5    1

Miles

the right fork. If you do the loop you will return on this left trail. (If you are just doing the Ruckel Creek Trail, keep left here to reverse the second half of the loop.) The trail goes around the campground, passing through an amphitheater for fireside chats. A large sign reads, "Buck Point 3/4 mile."

From the Buck Point Trail 439 sign a well-maintained trail switchbacks uphill. After about 0.5 mile, the trees are succeeded by powerlines, and the trail crosses underneath them to reach Buck Point. Buck Point is not terribly scenic due to the powerlines, but having an official destination enables the trail to remain maintained up to this point. This can be the end of the trip, if all you want is a short walk with a view, but Wauna Viewpoint is a little better in the view department.

Head south, past Buck Point, and stay right. The trail drops slightly onto a rocky mossy slope. The trail climbs through this slide area. Stay left, heading east, as you climb. Several cairns, or large piles of rocks, mark the faint trail. The trail climbs back up to the crest of the ridge, then turns straight up the ridge before reaching the base of a cliff. Then the trail skirts left around it. The trail is very steep, but there are roots and small trees to pull yourself up with.

 Warning: this trail requires scrambling on all fours.

*Bridge of the Gods from the Ruckel Creek Trail.*

You ought to get used to climbing up a steep trail on top of the ridge, because the trail continues to do this for the next 2.5 miles. In several spots you have to scramble up and down large rocks. There is one scary stretch that crosses a section of the rocky ridge just 4 feet wide.

There are several good viewpoints along the way. From the ridge you can see Table Mountain, Hamilton Mountain, Tanner Butte, and Mount St. Helens if it is clear and the "mountains are out." The last stretch is also steep and the trail is marked only by blazes.

As the grade flattens out, the trail crosses Ruckel Creek. There is no bridge. This is a good place to filter water because the trail down Ruckel Creek doesn't get very close to the creek. The forest is composed of mostly middle-aged hemlock and fir trees and well shaded.

Shortly after Ruckel Creek, climb up and to the left. A faint trail leads to the junction with the Ruckel Creek Trail 405, where you have two choices. Right leads onto the Benson Plateau and further on to the Pacific Crest Trail 2000. Turn left to complete the loop. The Ruckel Creek Trail is well-maintained and easy to follow.

Next is the steady descent into Ruckel Creek valley. About 2 miles down are several hanging gardens of flowers. The open green slopes offer a pleasant break from hiking in the trees.

After 6.5 miles of hiking, the trail drops on steep, short switchbacks, passing an excellent view of the Bridge of the Gods. The trail is very steep on this last section. If you decide to reverse the route or just hike up Ruckel Creek, be ready for this section to get you winded. It might even slow you to less than a 1 mile–per–hour hiking speed.

After many more switchbacks, the trail levels off across an open rocky area. It then descends in forested slopes to Ruckel Creek. Just after you've seen Ruckel Creek for the first time since the top of the hike, the trail intersects Gorge Trail 400 on the old scenic highway. Turn left on the stone bridge for the final 0.4 mile to the campground and back to the trailhead.

# PACIFIC CREST TRAIL (PCT)

**Overview:**

The Pacific Crest Trail National Scenic Trail 2000 (PCT) extends from Mexico to Canada, and encompasses miles of trail. The section through the Columbia River Gorge offers at least four good hiking options, more if you like. On the Oregon side, the best way to break the trail up is to make a short day hike from the Bridge of the Gods to Dry Creek Falls. For longer trips, try starting at Herman Creek for quicker access.

# *26   PACIFIC CREST TRAIL TO DRY CREEK FALLS*

|  |  |
|---|---|
| **General description:** | An easy hike to a little–known waterfall. |
| **Distance:** | 4.4 miles. |
| **Difficulty:** | Easy. |
| **Traffic:** | Moderate. |
| **Trail type:** | Well-maintained. |
| **Best season:** | May to October. |
| **Elevation change:** | 580 feet. |
| **Maximum elevation:** | 760 feet. |
| **Topographic maps:** | Carson USGS and Bonneville Dam Green Trails. |

**Finding the trailhead:** To reach the Pacific Crest Trail's Bridge of the Gods Trailhead, drive east from Portland on Interstate 84 and take Exit 44 at Cascade Locks. Follow the off–ramp toward the town, and just as you pass under the steel girders of the Bridge of the Gods, turn right and then right again into the parking lot before the toll booth. The trail starts to the south, across the road.

**Key points:**
    0.2   Junction with Gorge Trail 400
    2.0   Junction with jeep road at bridge over Dry Creek
    2.2   Dry Creek Falls

# PACIFIC CREST TRAIL TO DRY CREEK FALLS

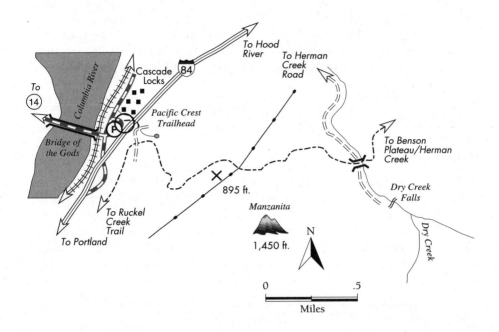

The trail: The Pacific Crest Trail 2000 is one of the best known trails in the Gorge. This particular section of the PCT is part of a longer route to the Benson Plateau; hence it is more efficient to start at the Herman Creek Work Center for extended trips. This short section does, however, offer a hidden waterfall without the crowds of the other Gorge waterfalls.

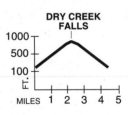

From the trailhead, cross the street and follow Trail 2000 under the interstate and up a road to the right, just under the overpass. One hundred yards up the road is the junction with Gorge Trail 400 and the PCT 2000. Turn left, heading east, on Trail 2000 leading into the trees. This area was the site of some interesting vandalism, which involved decorating trail signs with underwear, the last time I passed through. It may not be as entertaining now.

The trail runs uphill slightly but is mostly level. The forest of young trees muffles the sounds of the interstate rather quickly. Familiar banana slugs dot the trail.

At 2 miles, the PCT 2000 reaches the junction with old Trail 405D to Ruckel Creek. You will not notice this junction without looking hard for it. It is just before you reach a gravel road. I don't recommend trying this route to Ruckel Creek unless your route finding skills are quite refined.

Instead, take a right, heading south, on the gravel road just before the bridge. A short distance later you'll find a little falls above the trail and an old water regulating gate. Dry Creek Falls is a single spout of water less than 50 feet tall. It is not the most spectacular falls in the area, but it isn't on the map and therefore not in most people's travel plans. Think of it as your own private waterfall.

Return to the trailhead via the same route or access areas further on the PCT 2000.

## 27   PACIFIC CREST TRAIL TO WHATUM LAKE

|  |  |
|---|---|
| **General description:** | A difficult overnight route with loop options back onto the Herman Creek Trail. |
| **Distance:** | 14.2 miles. |
| **Difficulty:** | Difficult. |
| **Traffic:** | Moderate. |
| **Trail type:** | Well-maintained. |
| **Best season:** | June to October. |
| **Elevation gain:** | 4,120 feet. |
| **Maximum elevation:** | 4,280 feet. |
| **Topographic maps:** | Carson, Whatum Lake USGS and Bonneville Dam Green Trails. |

**Finding the trailhead:** You have two possible routes to the start of this trail. The best way is to take Interstate 84 east from Portland to the weigh station exit, just after Cascade Locks Exit 44. Drive through the weigh station area and turn right onto Herman Creek Road. Follow the road for 2 miles to the well-marked Herman Creek Recreation Site. This is the work station for trail maintenance in the Columbia Gorge. If you miss the weigh station, take Herman Creek Road Exit 47, then turn right, heading west, for 0.5 mile to the Herman Creek Recreation Site on the south side of the road. Drive up toward the campground, bearing right at the junction with the campground road. The trailhead is at the far end of the loop next to Pacific Crest Trail 2000 and Herman Creek Trail 406 signs. Bathrooms are available at the trailhead, along with ample parking.

Doing this hike as a point-to-point requires leaving a vehicle at Whatum Lake, or having someone pick you up there. To get to Whatum Lake, drive east to Hood River Exit 62 and turn right, following the signs to the city center on Oak. At the 13th Street stoplight turn right, heading south. Follow

# PACIFIC CREST TRAIL TO WHATUM LAKE

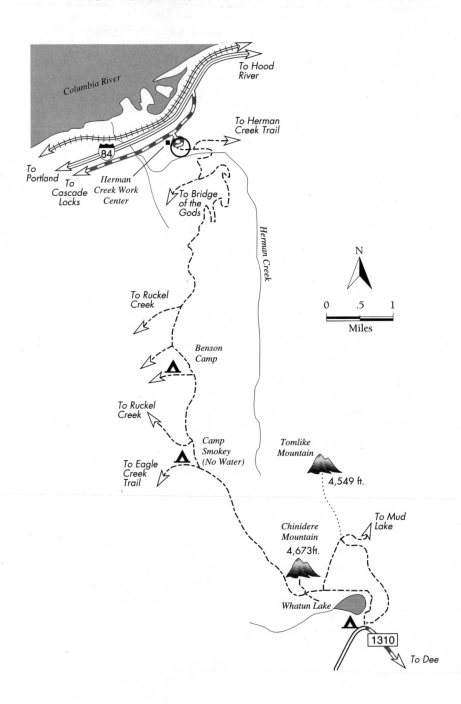

Columbia River

To Hood River

To Herman Creek Trail

84

To Portland

To Cascade Locks

Herman Creek Work Center

To Bridge of the Gods

Herman Creek

N

0 .5 1
Miles

To Ruckel Creek

Benson Camp

To Ruckel Creek

Camp Smokey (No Water)

Tomlike Mountain
4,549 ft.

To Eagle Creek Trail

To Mud Lake

Chinidere Mountain
4,673ft.

Whatun Lake

1310

To Dee

the main route. Stay left on Tucker Road, following the signs to Dee after bending left and right. At Dee, turn right onto Lost Lake Road, cross the railroad tracks, and stay left at the fork. Follow the well–marked paved Forest Road 1310 for 10 miles to the Whatum Lake trailhead, which is on your right.

**Key points:**

| | |
|---|---|
| 0.1 | Junction with trail to work center |
| 0.6 | Junction with Herman Bridge Trail 406E to PCT 2000 |
| 1.9 | Junction PCT 2000 |
| 5.4 | Teakettle Spring |
| 6.4 | Junction Benson Way Trail 405B |
| 7.1 | Junction with Benson-Ruckel Trail 405A |
| 7.8 | Junction with Ruckel Creek Trail 405 |
| 8.7 | Junction with Benson Plateau Trail 405B |
| 9.1 | Camp Smokey |
| 12.2 | Junction with Chinidere Mountain Trail |
| 12.4 | Junction with Herman Creek Trail 406 |
| 13.9 | Whatum Lake |
| 14.2 | Whatum Lake Trailhead |

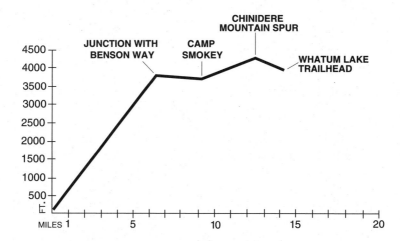

**The trail:** The Pacific Crest Trail 2000 is probably not the most popular trail in the Gorge, but it runs a close third behind Multnomah Falls and Eagle Creek. This particular section of the PCT 2000 is strenuous and dry, especially the climb from Herman Creek up to the Benson Plateau. There is not much water along the way, except for Teakettle Spring and the slightly out of the way Ruckel Creek, until Whatum Lake. The trail up, and the trail along the plateau, offer several views of the broken-topped forest of Herman Creek and majestic Tomlike Mountain Ridge.

From the trailhead, the trail drops slightly before one switchback and the

*Whatum Lake on a calm sunny day.*

first junction, which is unmarked. The trail on your right descends to the work center, the trail on your left continues to climb south up gradual switchbacks. The trail passes underneath powerlines and crosses a jeep road as it climbs.

At 0.6 mile is the junction with Herman Bridge Trail 406E. Stay right for the main trail; left is the Herman Creek Trail 406. This section technically is a shortcut to the PCT 2000 rather than starting in Cascade Locks Trailhead.

The trail drops crossing a bridge over Herman Creek and then climbs through maple and fir forest to a tallus slope at the junction with the PCT 2000.

After 1.9 miles, turn left, heading southwest on PCT 2000, and gently traverse the slope towards the Herman Creek valley before starting the steep climb up the ridge. The next 4.5 miles of climbing gains 2,940 feet, but it's nothing compared to the Starvation Ridge Hike. Still, it's more than most of the population is fit for. Bring water: it's 3.5 miles from the junction to Teakettle Spring.

Before you reach Teakettle Spring there are several small, flat lookouts that could possibly harbor a tent, if you're willing to walk at least 0.5 mile to the spring for water.

At 5.4 miles is Teakettle Spring. It had clear water when visited in late September, but you can expect a little mud-lined pool about three feet in diameter when you arrive. You probably will not care, because thirst and

*Mount Hood from Chinidere Mountain.*

iodine do mix.

After Teakettle Spring, Trail 2000 continues to climb up to the plateau into a forest of mountain hemlock. Soon after the trail levels out, at 6.4 miles, is the junction with Benson Way Trail 405B.

If you wish to camp soon and don't have much water, I recommend taking a right for Ruckel Creek. Ruckel Creek has several good campsites and water almost year–round, but don't count on it late in the season, and if you push on to Camp Smokey you're unlikely to find water. One site is right at the junction with Ruckel Creek Trail 405, and is called Hunters Camp on the Gorge map. It has room for 3-4 tents and a fire ring. You can return to the PCT by continuing south on Trails 405B or C.

At 7.1 miles is the next junction. Next on Trail 2000, past Benson Way junction, is the junction with Benson Ruckel Trail 405A. This trail is faint and little used, probably because most travelers decide to go to Ruckel Creek earlier on and don't rejoin the PCT until the other end of Benson Plateau.

The junction with Ruckel Creek Trail 405, at 7.8 miles, is another opportunity to turn right for a camp spot. The Benson Camp is the last campsite near water before Whatum Lake.

At 8.7 miles, after a brief view to the east, the last Benson Plateau Trail 405B joins the PCT. Trail 405B is a fairly well–used path, and many of the hikers that camp at Ruckel Creek use it to return to the PCT 2000.

At 9.1 miles is Camp Smokey and the junction with Eagle-Benson Trail 434, which receives relatively light use by hikers descending to Eagle Creek.

Still, it's not too hard to follow. There is room for 2-3 tents and an established fire ring. Camp Smokey is rumored to have a spring, but I did not find any water there when I arrived. I would recommend camping on the Benson Plateau or at least getting your water there.

Stay left after Camp Smokey and follow the trail as it breaks out of the trees around an old, burned ridgetop. One of the benefits of the burn is the excellent views of Tomlike Mountain to the east and Tanner Butte to the west.

As the trail re-enters the dense forest it starts to climb steadily. There is not much of a view until just before the spur trail to Chinidere Mountain. You can see up the open slope of the mountain, but don't try to scramble up because there is a well-maintained trail just a few hundred yards further.

At mile 12.2 is the marked junction with the trail to the top of Chinidere Mountain. Turn left for the climb or skip it and continue straight to Whatum Lake. It is about 0.5 mile to the top of Chinidere Mountain on steep switchbacks. The top is composed of loose rock, and several wind shelters built by previous visitors are obvious. The view from Chinidere Mountain of Mount Hood is one of the best in the Scenic Area, but that is not all that you can see. Mount Defiance and the Washington Cascades are also visible.

Once back down on the main trail 0.2 mile later is the junction with the Herman Creek Trail 406. Stay right for Whatum Lake unless you plan to complete a loop back to Herman Creek.

**Note:** You can continue on the PCT to Mount Hood. See *Hiking Oregon's Mount Hood and Badger Creek Wildernesses* (Falcon 1998) by Fred Barstad.

# HERMAN CREEK AREA

**Overview:**

Herman Creek is a good area to hike in because the old growth forest and the many trails help keep hiker density down, even when the trailhead parking lot is full. Several loop options exist here; two of the best are the Indian Point Loop from the Gorton Creek Trail, and the Casey Creek Loop. The best extended trip is up to the Benson Plateau and back on the PCT. For a simple overnight also consider a trip to Cedar Swamp.

# 28 HERMAN CREEK TRAIL TO WHATUM LAKE

| | |
|---|---|
| **General description:** | A good overnight route with loop options back on the Benson Plateau. |
| **Distance:** | 12.1 miles. |
| **Difficulty:** | Intermediate. |
| **Traffic:** | Moderate to heavy. |
| **Trail type:** | Maintained. |
| **Best season:** | Late May through October. |
| **Elevation gain:** | 3,800 feet. |
| **Maximum elevation:** | 3,960 feet. |
| **Topographic maps:** | Carson, Whatum Lake USGS and Bonneville Dam Green Trails. |

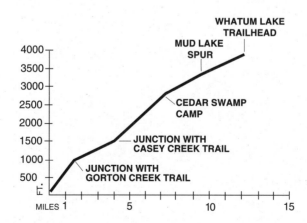

**Finding the trailhead:** From Portland, take Interstate 84 east to the weigh station exit just after Cascade Locks Exit 44. Drive through the weigh

# HERMAN CREEK TRAIL TO WHATUM LAKE

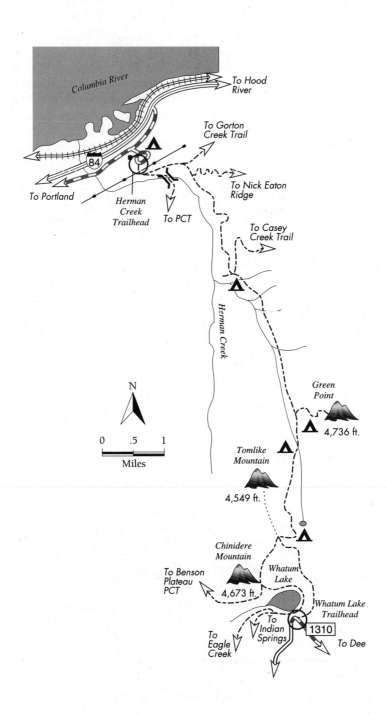

Columbia River

To Hood River

To Gorton Creek Trail

84

To Portland

Herman Creek Trailhead

To PCT

To Nick Eaton Ridge

To Casey Creek Trail

Herman Creek

N

0 .5 1
Miles

Green Point
4,736 ft.

Tomlike Mountain
4,549 ft.

Chinidere Mountain
4,673 ft.

Whatum Lake

To Benson Plateau PCT

Whatum Lake Trailhead

1310

To Dee

To Indian Springs

To Eagle Creek

station area and turn right on Herman Creek. Follow the road for 2 miles to the well-marked Herman Creek Recreation Site. If you miss the weigh station exit, or are coming from Hood River, take Herman Creek Road Exit 47, then turn right, heading west for 0.5 mile to the Herman Creek Recreation Site on the south side of the road. Drive up toward the campground, keeping right at the junction with the campground road. The trailhead is at the far end of the loop, next to a Pacific Crest Trail 2000 sign. Bathrooms are available at the trailhead along with ample parking.

To make the trip one way, you must leave a vehicle at Whatum Lake or arrange to be picked up there. Drive east to Hood River Exit 62 and turn right. Follow the signs toward the city center on Oak. At the 13th Street stoplight turn right, heading south on the main route. Stay left on Tucker Road and follow the signs to Dee. At Dee, turn right onto Lost Lake Road, cross some railroad tracks, and stay left at the fork. Follow the well-marked, paved route for 10 miles to Whatum Lake Trailhead, which will be on your right.

**Key points:**
- 0.1 Junction with trail to work center
- 0.6 Junction with Herman Bridge Trail 406E
- 0.8 Unmarked junction with old logging roads
- 1.4 Marked clearing junction with Gorton Creek Trail 408 and Gorge Trail 400.
- 1.5 Junction with Nick Eaton Trail 447
- 4.0 Junction with Casey Creek Trail 476
- 7.3 Cedar Swamp Camp
- 9.2 Junction with trail to Mud Lake
- 10.1 Junction with Anthill Trail 406B
- 12.1 Whatum Lake Trailhead

**The trail:** Herman Creek is known for its old growth fir and cedar forest. The best trees are past the Casey Creek junction. For an overnight stay amongst the cedars, hike to Cedar Swamp and spend a night, or continue on to Mud Lake for a second night. You can either end your hike at Whatum Lake or loop back on the Benson Plateau via the Pacific Crest Trail 2000 (PCT). Several easy mountain climbs along the way include Chinidere and Tomlike mountains.

From the trailhead, the trail descends slightly before you reach a switchback and the first junction, unmarked. Stay left as the trail continues to climb on switchbacks. After you pass underneath some powerlines you will cross a jeep road, keeping straight south.

At 0.6 mile is the next junction with the Herman Bridge Trail 406E to Pacific Crest Trail 2000. Stay left, heading south. Trail 406 becomes more roadlike as you proceed. There are no real views of Herman Creek until the Casey Creek Trail junction, where a spur trail leads to a lookout above the creek.

Next, pass an unmarked junction where several old roads meet. Keep

*Mud Lake in the fall.*

heading due south, bearing straight and to the right. At 1.4 miles is the clearing junction with Gorge Trail 400, Gorton Creek Trail 408, and Herman Creek Trail 406. Stay right, heading south on the main Herman Creek Trail 406. The trail is broad and level.

Just 0.1 mile farther is a junction with Nick Eaton Ridge Trail 447. Stay right. Continuing on the Herman Creek Trail, the grade is gentle, almost flat. The sound of Herman Creek muffles any residual sound from the interstate. After passing some Oregon oak, the trail climbs more steadily to a cascading falls about 60 feet high. Crossing the stream below the falls is not hard, but another stream 0.5 mile further along the trail is likely to get your feet wet. At 1.5 miles from the junction, another cascade crosses the trail, but this is an easy ford.

The Casey Creek Trail 476 junction is on your left after 4 miles, just before a campsite on the right. There is not much of a view. A water source is farther along on Herman Creek Trail 406. To get a look at Herman Creek, you have to hike down a spur trail. It is to the right as you push west through the campsite area for 0.3 mile to a lookout. The whitewater is still 50 feet below.

Past Casey Creek junction, the trail climbs gradually uphill through increasingly dense old growth forest. At 7.3 miles is the Cedar Swamp Camp, where, unsurprisingly, there are quite a few large cedars. Several tent sites

*The route up Tomlike Mountain from Herman Creek Trail.*

make enough room for multiple camping parties. There are signs of heavy use and several fire rings. A water source runs conveniently through the camp. If Cedar Swamp does not suit you, there are a couple of smaller sites about 0.5 mile farther.

Past Cedar Swamp, the trail fords Herman Creek and begins to climb through even more overgrown forest. A couple of open spots provide views of the forested slopes of the Herman Creek Valley.

At 9.2 miles is a marked junction; turn left, heading east, onto a spur trail if you want to visit Mud Lake. The 0.3 mile trail down to Mud Lake is less maintained than Trail 406, but not too hard to follow. However, there are few tent sites. It would be difficult to get more than two tents on flat ground here. The campsite is back out of sight of the lake. Mud Lake is boggy, but offers a nice view of the tallus slopes to the east, where the vine maple is awfully pretty in its fall colors.

Past the Mud Lake junction, the trail continues to climb more steeply on switchbacks. At the crest of the climb, just before the junction with the Anthill Trail 406B, an unmarked path on your right leads off to the north.

This path is the beginning of an off-trail route to the top of Tomlike Mountain. If you want to make the ascent, hug the east edge of the ridge, staying on top until you get a view of the mountain. Then follow the ridge line over boulders, subalpine fir, and open meadows to the top. Give yourself about two hours to make the side trip.

Fifty feet beyond the Tomlike Mountain Trail (10.1 miles on the main trail) is the junction with the Anthill Trail 406B to Whatum Lake Trailhead. If you left a vehicle there or plan to camp, hang a left. Whatum Lake has brook trout and several good campsites, but gets heavy use from the Eagle Creek Trail and the PCT.

Herman Creek Trail 406 continues to the right for Chinidere Mountain and the Pacific Crest Trail 2000. About 0.2 mile later is an unmarked trail on your left; stay right. As another, well-maintained trail comes in from the left, continue to keep right, heading west. At 11.1 miles the Herman Creek Trail ends at the junction with the Pacific Crest Trail. Stay right for the PCT and Tomlike Mountain. Left takes you to Whatum Lake.

---

## BENSON PLATEAU LOOP OPTION:

In order to make this an extended trip, longer than one or two nights, follow a loop route from the Herman Creek Trail 406 to the Pacific Crest Trail 2000 and back to the work center via Benson Plateau.

If you don't have any water you'd better go down to Whatum Lake and fill up, because there is no water on the PCT until the upper reaches of Ruckel Creek at Benson Camp. Don't count on water at Camp Smokey. There is a marked junction 0.2 mile past the trail to Whatum Lake with the trail to the top of Chinidere Mountain. It is about 0.5 mile to the top of Chinidere Mountain on steep switchbacks. The top is loose rock and several wind shelters built by previous visitors are obvious. The view of Mount Hood from Chinidere Mountain is one of the best in the scenic area, but that is not all that you can see. Mount Defiance and the Washington Cascades are also visible.

Once back down on the main trail, to complete the loop continue right on the PCT toward the Benson Plateau. Follow the Pacific Crest Trail 2000 back to the Herman Creek Work Station and camp at Benson Camp or Ruckel Creek, depending upon whether there is still water at Benson Camp late in the season. Ruckel Creek holds water year-round. See Hike 27 for the Pacific Crest Trail.

| | |
|---|---|
| **General description:** | A healthy day hike with a good climb up Nick Eaton Ridge from the Herman Creek Trail. |
| **Distance:** | 11.2 miles. |
| **Difficulty:** | Difficult. |
| **Traffic:** | Moderate to light. |
| **Trail type:** | Maintained. |
| **Best season:** | June to October. |
| **Elevation gain:** | 3,840 feet. |
| **Maximum elevation:** | 4,000 feet. |
| **Topographic maps:** | Carson USGS and Bonneville Dam Green Trails. |

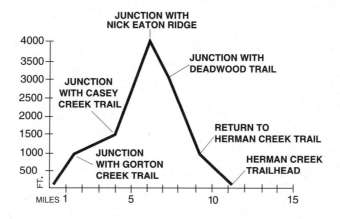

**Finding the trailhead:** From Portland, take Interstate 84 east to the weigh station exit just after Cascade Locks Exit 44. Drive through the weigh station area and turn right, heading east, onto Herman Creek Road. Follow the road for 2 miles to the well-marked Herman Creek Recreation Site. This is the work station for much of the trail maintenance in the Columbia Gorge.

If you miss the weigh station exit, or are coming from Hood River, take the Herman Creek Road Exit 47, then turn right, heading west, for 0.5 mile to the Herman Creek Recreation Site, on the south side of the road. Drive up toward the campground, keeping right at the junction with the campground road. The trailhead is at the far end of the loop next to a Pacific Crest Trail sign. Bathrooms are available at the trailhead, along with ample parking.

# CASEY CREEK LOOP

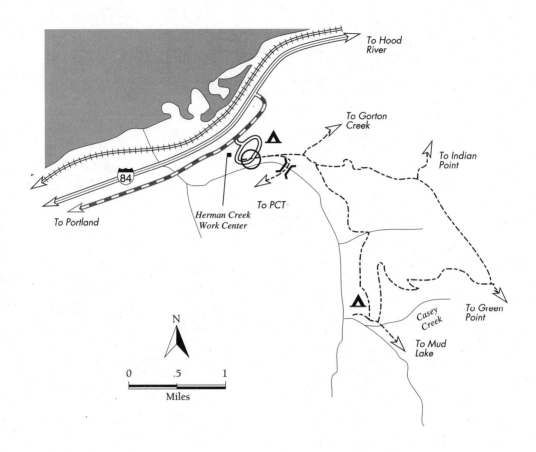

**Key points:**

- 0.1 Junction with trail to work center
- 0.6 Junction with trail to Pacific Crest National Scenic Trail 2000
- 0.8 Unmarked junction with old logging roads
- 1.4 Marked clearing junction with Herman Creek Trail 406 and Gorge Trail 400
- 4.0 Junction with Casey Creek Trail 467
- 6.1 Junction with Nick Eaton Ridge Trail 447
- 7.3 Junction with Deadwood Trail
- 7.8 Junction with Ridge Cutoff Trail 437 to Indian Point

**The trail:** The Casey Creek Loop is an 11.2 mile day hike, with an overnight option at the Casey Creek Trail junction. The climb up to Nick Eaton

Ridge is not easy, but the hiker is rewarded with great views across the valley to the Benson Plateau.

From the trailhead, Trail 406 drops slightly before reaching one switchback and the first junction, unmarked. Stay left; the trail continues south, climbing gradually on switchbacks. Then pass underneath some powerlines and cross a jeep road, keeping straight.

At 0.6 miles you'll reach the next junction with Herman Bridge Trail 406E to Pacific Crest Trail 2000. Stay left, and watch for wild strawberries on the uphill side of the trail. Trail 406 becomes more roadlike as you progress. You can hear Herman Creek burbling off to your right, but there won't be much of a view of the creek until you reach the Casey Creek Trail 467 Junction.

Next, pass an unmarked junction where several old roads meet. Keep heading straight and to the right. At 1.4 miles is the large clearing junction, where Gorge Trail 400 (on your left), Gorton Creek Trail 408 (on your left and straight, to the southeast), and Herman Creek Trail 406 (to your right, following the main road) all meet.

Take the Herman Creek Trail 406 heading south, which continues to the right on a wide trail. At 0.1 mile past the junction is another junction, with the Nick Eaton Ridge Trail 447. You can do the loop either way. If you are eager to climb, turn left. If you want to climb later, stay right. Farther on the Herman Creek Trail 406, the grade is gentle, almost level. The sound of Herman Creek muffles any residual sound from the interstate. After passing some Oregon oak and blooming lupine, the trail climbs more steadily to a cascading falls about 60 feet high. Crossing the stream below the falls is not hard, but another stream 0.5 mile further down the trail is likely to get your feet wet. Around 1.5 miles from the last two junctions, another cascade crosses the trail which is easily forded.

At 4.0 miles you'll reach a junction with the Casey Creek Trail 467 on your left, just before a campsite appears on your right, a bit further along Herman Creek Trail 406. To get a look at Herman Creek, you have to hike down a spur trail through the campsite area for 0.3 mile to a lookout 50 feet above the whitewater of the creek. The camp has a few cedars, but large Douglas-fir and dense, younger western hemlocks predominate.

Turn left up Casey Creek Trail.

 Always filter or carry plenty of water prior to a lengthy climb.

Water is seasonally available 0.1 miles past the junction on Trail 406. The Casey Creek Trail is very steep and dry; no water is available, despite its namesake. Several spots offer views of Tomlike Mountain and the Benson Plateau. The last stretch to the top is almost completely vertical. Once you get to the top, you might want to hang right for a 0.1 mile walk to a craggy open space, where you can get a good view of Mount Adams. Then retrace your steps to take the left trail onto Nick Eaton Ridge Trail 447. The trail follows the ridge down with several fine viewpoints. Leave the Columbia Wilderness at Deadwood Junction.

It's 0.5 mile down to the Gorton Creek Trail 408; you can turn here for more miles, but I would stay straight on Nick Eaton Ridge Trail 447. After a nice view of Mount Hood you'll reach the junction with the Ridge Cutoff Trail 437. It is 0.8 mile farther to use Gorton Creek Trail 406 and Indian Point. If you want to extend the trip a little make the side trip to Indian Point. Without making the trip to Indian Point, keep left on Nick Eaton Ridge Trail 447 to rejoin Herman Creek Trail 406, which leads back to the trailhead.

## 30   INDIAN POINT LOOP

| | |
|---|---|
| **General description:** | A good day hike loop up around Nick Eaton Ridge, with spectacular views of the Gorge. |
| **Distance:** | 8.4 miles. |
| **Difficulty:** | Difficult. |
| **Traffic:** | Heavy. |
| **Trail type:** | Maintained |
| **Best season:** | Late May to October. |
| **levation gain:** | 2,720 feet. |
| **Maximum elevation:** | 2,880 feet. |
| **Topographic maps:** | Mount Defiance USGS and Hood River Green Trails. |

**Finding the trailhead:** From Portland, take Interstate 84 east to the weigh station exit, just after Cascade Locks Exit 44. Drive through the weigh station area and turn right, heading east, onto Herman Creek Road. Follow the road for 2 miles to the sign for Herman Creek Recreation Site.

If you miss the weigh station exit, or are coming from Hood River, take Herman Creek Road Exit 47. Then turn right, heading west, for 0.5 mile to reach the Herman Creek Recreation Site on the south side of the road. Drive right up to the campground, keeping right at the junction with the campground road. The trailhead is at the far end of the loop, next to the Pacific Crest Trail 2000. Bathrooms are available at the trailhead, along with ample parking.

# INDIAN POINT LOOP

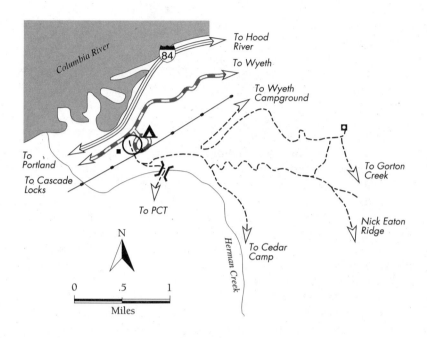

## Key points:

- 0.1 Junction with trail to work center
- 0.6 Junction with Herman Bridge Trail 406E to the PCT 2000
- 0.8 Unmarked junction with old logging roads
- 1.4 Marked clearing junction with Gorton Creek Trail 408 and Gorge Trail 400
- 4.0 Junction with Nick Eaton Cutoff Trail 437/Indian Point
- 5.0 Junction with Nick Eaton Ridge Trail 447
- 7.0 Return to Herman Creek Trail 406

**The trail:** Gorton Creek Trail passes through old growth Douglas-fir trees, and offers multiple views of the Gorge and the cascades to the north. For day hiking, the best route is a hike to Indian Point. Take the Ridge Cutoff Trail and return on Nick Eaton Trail 447.

From the trailhead, the trail dips slightly, then climbs on switchbacks. Stay left at the first,

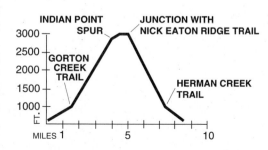

unmarked junction, heading south as the trail continues to climb gradually on switchbacks. After seeing some powerlines, cross a jeep road and continue straight, due south. The disturbed area under the powerlines offers ideal germination sites for invasive species like Himalayan blackberry and Scotch broom. Past the powerlines, the vegetation tends toward snowberry and thimbleberry, both native species.

At 0.6 mile you'll reach a junction with the Herman Bridge Trail 406E to the PCT. Keep left, continuing south, as the trail becomes more roadlike.

Next is an unmarked junction with several old roads; continue straight and to the right. The forest here is in early succession, densely packed with young trees. There is little vegetation on the excessively shaded forest floor. This area offers a nice contrast to the old growth forest further up the trail, where the vegetation is lush and the density of trees low.

At 1.4 miles is the clearing junction, where Gorge Trail 400 (on your left), Gorton Creek Trail 408 (on your left and straight, to the southeast), and Herman Creek Trail 406 (to your right, following the main road) all meet. Take Gorton Creek Trail 408. After leaving the junction, the trees will be older than those you've seen previously; they are fewer in number but much larger. The forest floor teems with common bushy plants like young vine maple. The trail is cool and shady as it climbs gradually through this old growth forest on a series of switchbacks.

At about 2.9 miles the trail crosses a seasonal creek; you might be able to filter water here, but don't count on it, especially late in the season. At 4 miles from the trailhead is the junction with the Ridge Cutoff Trail 437 from the Nick Eaton Ridge Trail. Before you take it, go 40 feet past the junction of the Gorton Creek Trail to the spur trail to Indian Point. It is a short, steep, descent to the top of a prominent rock structure for excellent views.

Go back to the Ridge Cutoff Trail 437 and turn southwest. After a short, gradual climb to the Nick Eaton Ridge Trail 447, turn right, heading north, on this well-maintained trail, which descends steeply on switchbacks to the Herman Creek Trail 406. Turn right again, continuing north, to the trailhead.

| | |
|---|---|
| **General description:** | A one- or two-day backpack climb up around Nick Eaton Ridge, with great views, dark forest corridors, and a clear, freshwater wilderness destination. |
| **Distance:** | 10.8 miles. |
| **Difficulty:** | Difficult. |
| **Traffic:** | Moderate. |
| **Trail type:** | Maintained |
| **Best season:** | Late May to October. |
| **Elevation gain:** | 4,576 feet. |
| **Maximum elevation:** | 4,736 feet. |
| **Topographic maps:** | Mount Defiance USGS; Hood River Green Trails. |

**Finding the trailhead:** From Portland, take Interstate 84 east to the weigh station exit just after Cascade Locks Exit 44. Drive through the weigh station area and turn right onto Herman Creek Road. Follow the road for 2 miles to a sign for the Herman Creek Recreation Site. If you miss the weigh station exit, or are coming from Hood River, take Herman Creek Road Exit 47. Then turn right, heading west, for 0.5 mile to the Herman Creek Recreation Site on the south side of the road. Drive up toward the campground, keeping right at the junction with the campground road. The trailhead is at the far end of the loop, next to signs for the Pacific Crest Trail (PCT) and the Herman Creek Trail.

To leave a car at the North Lake Trailhead, drive east to Hood River Exit 62, turn right, and follow the signs toward the city center on Oak. At the 13th Street stoplight turn right, heading south, and follow the main route. Stay left on Tucker Road, following the signs to Dee. At Dee, turn right onto Lost Lake Road, cross some railroad tracks, and turn right onto Punch Bowl Road. Green Road veers to the left 0.2 mile later but keep right, heading north. After 1 mile, turn left onto Dead Point Road, heading west up Dead Point Creek on Forest Road 2820.

At 7.5 miles is a junction with FR 620; stay left on FR 2820. At 9.4 miles is another junction with FR 2821, but stay left, heading west on 2820. At 12.6 miles from Dee is an unmarked junction with a less well-maintained road on your right. Take this right fork on the north side of the road, and 0.2 mile later you'll reach the Rainy Lake picnic area and the trailhead. If you continue on FR 2820, it dead-ends next to Black Lake; if you reach the lake you've gone too far.

## Key points:
- 0.1   Junction with trail to work center
- 0.6   Junction with Herman Bridge Trail 406E to PCT 2000
- 0.8   Unmarked junction with old logging roads
- 1.4   Marked clearing junction with Herman Creek Trail 406 and Gorge Trail 400

# GORTON CREEK TRAIL TO RAINY LAKE

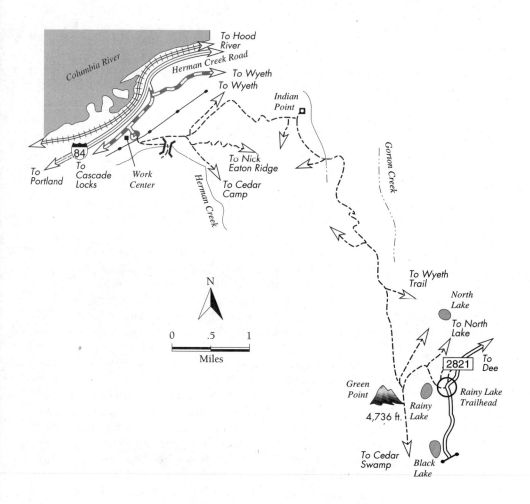

| 4.0 | Junction with Nick Eaton Cutoff Trail 437/Indian Point |
| 4.8 | Junction with Deadwood Trail |
| 7.4 | Junction with Nick Eaton Ridge Trail 447 |
| 8.0 | Junction with Green Point Cutoff Trail 412 |
| 9.5 | Green Point Junction with Trail 423 to Rainy Lake and Herman Creek Cutoff Trail 410 and Green Point Ridge Trail 418 |
| 10.1 | Junction with trail to North Lake |
| 10.8 | Rainy Lake Campground |

**The trail:** Gorton Creek Trail passes through a forest of old growth Douglas-fir trees and offers multiple views of the Gorge and the cascades to the

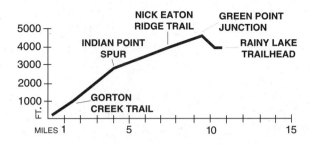

North. For day hiking, the best route is the hike to Indian Point. Take the Ridge Cutoff Trail and return on Nick Eaton Trail 447. (See Indian Point Loop).

From the trailhead, Trail 406 dips slightly, then climbs on switchbacks. Stay left at the first, unmarked junction, heading south as the trail continues to climb gradually on switchbacks. After seeing some powerlines, cross a jeep road and continue straight, due south. The disturbed area under the powerlines offers ideal germination sites for invasive species like Himalayan blackberry and Scotch broom. Past the powerlines, the vegetation tends toward snowberry and thimbleberry, both native species.

At 0.6 mile you'll reach a junction with the Herman Bridge Trail 406E to the PCT. Keep left, continuing south, as Trail 406 becomes more roadlike.

Next is an unmarked junction with several old roads; continue straight and to the right. The forest here is in early succession, densely packed with young trees. There is little vegetation on the excessively shaded forest floor. This area offers a nice contrast to the old growth forest further up the trail, where the vegetation is lush and the density of trees low.

At 1.4 miles is the clearing junction, where Gorge Trail 400 (on your left), Gorton Creek Trail 408 (on your left and straight, to the southeast), and Herman Creek Trail 406 (to your right, following the main road) all meet. Take Gorton Creek Trail 408. After leaving the junction, the trees will be older than those you've seen previously; they are fewer in number but much larger. The forest floor teems with common bushy plants like young vine maple. The trail is cool and shady as it climbs gradually through this old growth forest on a series of switchbacks.

At about 2.9 miles, Trail 408 crosses a seasonal creek; you might be able to filter water here, but don't count on it, especially late in the season. At 4 miles from the trailhead is the junction with the Ridge Cutoff Trail 437 from the Nick Eaton Ridge Trail 447. Go 40 feet past the junction of the Gorton Creek trail to the spur trail to Indian Point. It is a short, steep, descent to the top of a prominent rock structure for excellent views.

Continue southeast on the Gorton Creek Trail 408, past the Indian Point spur, until the junction with the Deadwood Trail, which climbs steeply to Nick Eaton Ridge and offers loop options to Casey Creek and Herman Creek trails (see the Casey Creek Loop Hike). Stay left at the Deadwood junction

113

and hop across a small stream. To your left is the first decent campsite.

 In order to reduce camping impact, it is better to use an already heavily impacted area than to trample the plants in an unused area.

Deadwood Camp gets heavy use and may already be occupied. It has a fire ring and cut logs to sit on beneath large firs which offer cool shade. The next possible campsite is about 1.5 miles further, but is much less desirable and might not have water.

The trail past Deadwood climbs around the ridge, then traverses across open tallus slopes with good views of the Gorge. At the second or third opening you can hear rushing water underneath the rocks, and an opening allows limited access to the source. Farther into the trees, the ground is just flat enough for a couple of tents, and with this water source provides a possible campsite. The next campsite is past the junction with the Nick Eaton Ridge Trail 447 and also has limited access to water.

The trail climbs steeply on switchbacks for another 1.1 miles to the junction with the Nick Eaton Ridge Trail 447. When you reach this point, you have done most, but not all of your climbing. Stay left, continuing south; just after this junction the trail levels out. A plateau-like area to the right offers good tent sites for several parties at least. Getting water requires a trek down to Gorton Creek to the left, but this is manageable. The lodgepole pine covering does not offer much protection from the rain, but does break much of the wind's force. Through the trees to your left you can see the Gorton Creek Valley and a little of the Gorge beyond.

After this flat stretch, Trail 408 switchbacks up again to a signed junction. The Green Point Ridge Cutoff Trail 418 is faintly visible to your left, but stay right and south on the Gorton Creek Trail 408. It winds upward gradually and then levels off into a corridor of middle-aged hemlocks. Often the trail is as straight as any hospital hallway. This corridor effect gives the area a medieval, "black forest" feeling, and you can imagine knights in tarnished armor riding down the trail.

The trail travels south across the ridge to the Green Point junction at 9.5 miles. Due south is the Herman Creek Cutoff Trail 408 to the Herman Creek and Whatum Lake areas. They offer other loop options for longer trips. A sharp left leads to the Green Point Cutoff trail. The second left would take you to Rainy Lake and North Lake. Turn left, heading east on Trail 423 for Rainy Lake.

The trail, cut into the side of Green Point, descends gradually as it traverses north across rocky and forested slopes. I would tell you what the view is like, but it was raining so hard when I was there that I can't say for sure. You might see Rainy Lake from the trail.

At 10.1 miles is the junction with the trail to North Lake and to Wyeth Trail 411. Stay right, heading south for Rainy Lake. Rainy Lake is awfully pretty when there's sunshine. The fishing is not that bad either.

## WYETH LOOP OPTION:

An excellent loop option exists for a 2- to 3-day backpack to Wyeth Campground. For a shorter shuttle and longer hiking, consider turning north to North Lake instead of the 10.1 mile junction. North Lake can be dismal in poor weather, but it has several campsites with room for several parties. There are fishing opportunities, but not much room to back cast. The trail down to Wyeth descends gradually through trees, but does offer a couple of views. This option means leaving a vehicle at the Wyeth Campground. See the Wyeth Trail to North Lake Hike for more detailed information.

# 32  WYETH TRAIL TO NORTH LAKE

|  |  |
|---|---|
| **General description:** | A good day hike or overnight backpack trip. |
| **Distance:** | 6.2 miles. |
| **Difficulty:** | Moderate. |
| **Traffic:** | Moderate. |
| **Trail type:** | Maintained |
| **Best season:** | April through October. |
| **Elevation gain:** | 3,940 feet. |
| **Maximum elevation:** | 4,100 feet. |
| **Topographic maps:** | Mount Defiance and Carson USGS and Bonneville Dam an Hood River Green Trails. |

**Finding the trailhead:** From Portland, take Interstate 84 east to Exit 51 for Wyeth. Follow the off-ramp, turn right, then right again, heading west on Herman Creek Road for 0.2 mile. Wyeth Campground is on the left, to the south. If the gate is locked, park near the entrance without blocking the gate. Either hike or drive through the campground. Stay right past the

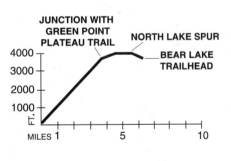

first two loops to the Gorton Creek Trailhead. There is ample parking, and public restrooms are located after the first loop in the campground.

To leave a car at Bear Lake Trailhead, drive east to Hood River Exit 62, turn right, and follow the signs toward city center on Oak. At the 13th Street stoplight turn right, heading south on the main route. Stay left on Tucker Road, following the signs to Dee. At Dee, turn right onto Lost Lake Road, cross some railroad tracks, and turn right onto Punch Bowl Road. Green Road veers off to the left 0.2 mile later, but stay right, heading north. After 1 mile, turn left onto Dead Point Road, heading west up Dead Point

# WYETH TRAIL TO NORTH LAKE

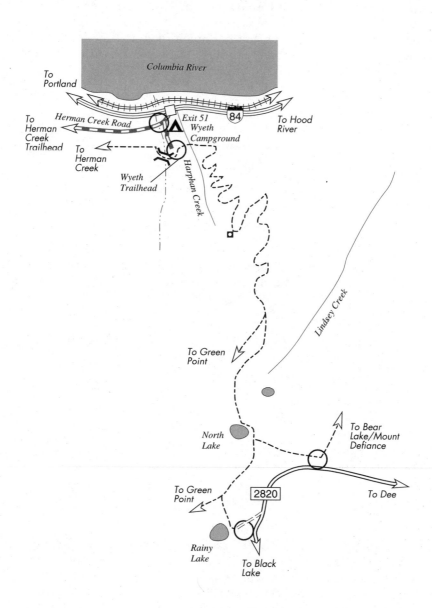

Creek on Forest Road 2820.

At 7.5 miles is FR 620; stay left on FR 2820. At 9.4 miles, pass the junction with FR 2821, keeping left (west) on 2820. At 11.7 miles, where there is an unmarked bend in the road to the left, a trailhead will be on the right, to the north, back from the road in the trees. Parking is avaiable on the south side of the road. If you continue on FR 2820 it dead-ends next to Black Lake, so if you've reached the lake, you've gone too far.

**Key points:**
- 0.1   Junction with Trail 400
- 3.8   Junction with Green Point Ridge Trail 418
- 5.5   Junction with spur trail to North Lake
- 6.2   Bear Lake Trailhead

**The trail:** Wyeth Trail 411 offers fishing, good views, old trees, and a solid workout. It can be either an out-and-back from Wyeth or a point-to-point hike. From the trailhead, the trail runs on a level grade for several hundred yards and soon reaches a junction with Gorge Trail 400. Stay left, heading east, for the Wyeth Trail 411. Straight ahead is an old road and a bridge to your right crosses Gorton Creek. The trail winds around the hillside above the campground and then passes under powerlines before reaching Harphan Creek. Ford the creek and continue straight. The trail climbs gradually but steadily on long switchbacks. There is not much of a view at this point.

After about 2 miles, cross a small stream to get your first good look at the elevation you've climbed. Then, continue to another lookout at the edge of Gorton Creek Valley, where you can see Carson City across the Gorge and Mount St. Helens some days.

There are several moss-covered openings with glacier lily and silky phacelia. At the Mark O. Hatfield Wilderness Boundary is a register. Filling out your permit is not required, but does provide USDA Forest Service information for hiker use.

As you crest the big climb, you'll see a lot of light through the trees on the left. You have almost made it to the Green Point Ridge Trail 418.

At the junction with the Green Point Ridge Trail 418, stay left, heading south, on the Wyeth Trail to North Lake. The trail proceeds gently, with a climb just before the lake. Cross Lindsey Creek before the junction with the Wyeth Trail 411 at the Bear Lake Trailhead. Turn right for North Lake. North Lake offers views of forested Green Point, and there are several good campsites on the lake. It is not that far from the Rainy Lake Campground and receives relatively heavy use. North Lake also contains fish.

From the junction with the North Lake spur, after spending the night, turn left, heading east, to Bear Lake Trailhead. The trail is mostly level, with a few slight ups and downs through middle-aged hemlock forest, for the 0.7 mile to the Bear Lake Trailhead.

*Ancient Douglas-firs highlight the Wyeth Trail.*

North Lake is close enough to Rainy Lake to warrant bringing some extra garbage bags to keep stuff dry.

Bear Lake Trailhead is kind of peculiar. It is easy to see the road from the trail, but hard to see the trail from the road. I sat there and watched several confused hiking parties drive by it several times before I waved to them.

If you did not leave a shuttle, follow the main trail back to the trailhead. Or consider a loop option with Gorton Creek Trail, Mount Defiance Trail or Herman Creek Trail.

# 33   LANCASTER FALLS

| | |
|---|---|
| **General description:** | A short hike to one of the Gorge's least-visited waterfalls, starting from spectacular Starvation Falls. |
| **Distance:** | 2.2 miles. |
| **Difficulty:** | Difficult. |
| **Traffic:** | Moderate. |
| **Trail type:** | Maintained. |
| **Best season:** | Year-round. |
| **Elevation gain:** | 280 feet. |
| **Maximum elevation:** | 400 feet. |
| **Topographic maps:** | Mount Defiance USGS and Hood River Green Trails. |

**Finding the trailhead:** From Portland, take Interstate 84 east to the Starvation Creek Rest Area, just after Wyeth Exit 51, heading east. If you get to Viento State Park, you have gone too far. The rest area is accessible only from the eastbound side. Mount Defiance Trail 413 starts on the right, just to the west, before the parking lot. Bathrooms are available at the trailhead.

### Key points:
    0.3   Junction with Starvation Ridge Cutoff Trail 414A
    1.0   Junction with Warren Creek Trail to Starvation Ridge Trail 414
    1.1   Lancaster Falls

**The trail:** The Mount Defiance Trail is known mostly for tough climbing, but the first section offers several waterfalls and requires little effort. On this short trip, you can pass Starvation Falls at the trailhead, Cabin Falls (out of sight), Hole-in-the-Wall Falls back from the trail, and Lancaster Falls on top of the trail.

The Starvation Creek Rest Area receives heavy use. It offers a short nature path to the bottom of Starvation Falls, which is worth a look. Starvation Creek got its name from the stranded train passengers that spent three weeks

# LANCASTER FALLS

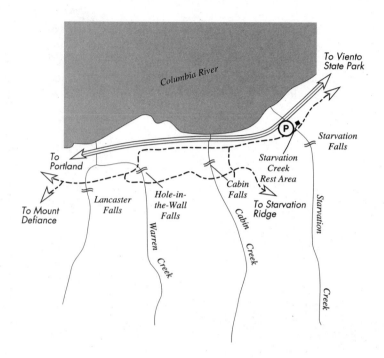

here in 1884. The falls crash down from a height of over 180 feet.

Start hiking on Mount Defiance Trail 413, which is found at the west end of the rest area. The path runs parallel to I-84 for 0.3 mile to the junction where the Starvation Ridge Cutoff Trail 414A forks to your left. Go straight, continuing west, on the Mount Defiance Trail.

After entering the trees the trail passes near Cabin Falls, which is not easily seen from the trail. Continue straight on the Mount Defiance Trail and cross a small footbridge below Hole-in-the-Wall Falls.

About 1 mile after you cross Warren Creek you'll reach the junction with the Starvation Ridge Trail to Warren Lake. Stay right, heading west, on Trail 413. The trail traverses the slope for another 0.1 mile before crossing underneath Lancaster Falls. Lancaster Falls is a series of cascades that rush over broken basalt, spreading across the trail and offering a welcome shower.

Return via the same route to the trailhead.

| General description: | A steep hike to Mount Defiance, with access to Warren Lake and North Lake loop options. |
|---|---|
| Distance: | 7.1 miles. |
| Difficulty: | Difficult. |
| Traffic: | Moderate to light. |
| Trail type: | Maintained. |
| Best season: | Late May to October. |
| Elevation gain: | 4,840 feet. |
| Maximum elevation: | 4,960 feet. |
| Topographic maps: | Mount Defiance USGS and Hood River Green Trails. |

**Finding the trailhead:** From Portland, take Interstate 84 east to the Starvation Creek Rest Area, just after Wyeth Exit 51, heading east. If you get to Viento State Park, you have gone too far. The rest area is accessible only from the eastbound side. Mount Defiance Trail 413 starts on the right, just to the west, before the parking lot. Bathrooms are available at the trailhead.

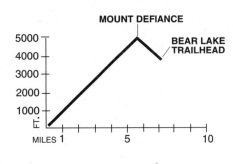

To leave a car at Bear Lake Trailhead, drive east to Hood River Exit 62, turn right, and follow the signs toward city center on Oak. At the 13th Street stoplight turn right, heading south on the main route. Stay left on Tucker Road, following the signs to Dee. At Dee, turn right onto Lost Lake Road, cross some railroad tracks, and turn right onto Punch Bowl Road. Green Road veers off to the left 0.2 mile later but stay right, heading north. After 1 mile, turn left onto Dead Point Road, heading west up Dead Point Creek on Forest Road 2820.

At 7.5 miles is FR 620; stay left on FR 2820. At 9.4 miles pass the junction with FR 2821, keeping left (west) on 2820. At 11.7 miles, where there is an unmarked bend in the road to the left, a trailhead will be on the right, to the north, back from the road in the trees. Parking is avaiable on the south side of the road. If you continue on FR 2820 it dead-ends next to Black Lake, so if you've reached the lake, you've gone too far.

**Key points:**

| 0.3 | Junction with Starvation Ridge Cutoff Trail 414A |
|---|---|
| 1.0 | Junction with Warren Creek Trail to Starvation Ridge Trail 414 |
| 1.1 | Lancaster Falls |
| 5.1 | Junction with Mitchell Point trail 417 to Warren Lake |
| 5.0 | Junction with steeper route to the top |

**The trail:** Local rumor has it that Mount Defiance is one of the toughest trails in Oregon, if not the toughest. After climbing it, a friend of mine was asked where he went. When he responded, his inquisitor asked if he had done it for training, because it is an even tougher hike than climbing Mount Hood from Timberline Lodge. Why else would you do it? We did it for fun. Judge for yourself how tough this trail is; I say it is not as hard as the Starvation Ridge Trail 414.

The top of Mount Defiance offers some of the best views of the Oregon and Washington cascades and the Hood River valley. It is 5.6 miles and 4,840 feet of elevation gain to the top. The trail switchbacks most of the way. At several points the grade levels out a bit, but generally the trail climbs straight up the ridge.

The Starvation Creek Rest Area receives heavy use. It has a short nature path to the bottom of Starvation Falls, which is worth a look. A water fountain along the way is a good place to fill water bottles.

Start hiking on Mount Defiance Trail 413, the beginning of which is at the west end of the rest area. The path runs parallel to Interstate 84 for 0.3 mile to a junction where Starvation Ridge Cutoff Trail 414A forks off to your left. Go straight, continuing west, on the Mount Defiance Trail.

After entering the trees, the trail passes near Cabin Falls, which is not easily seen from the trail. Continue straight on the Mount Defiance Trail 413. The path crosses a small footbridge across Warren Creek, below Hole-in-the-Wall Falls.

One mile after crossing Warren Creek you'll reach the junction with the Starvation Ridge Trail to Warren Lake. Stay right on Trail 413. The trail traverses the slope for 0.1 mile before crossing underneath Lancaster Falls. Lancaster Falls is a series of cascades that rush over broken basalt, spreading across the trail and offering a welcome shower. This is the last place to filter water for the steep climb ahead.

The trail advances around the ridge before starting upward on steep switchbacks. The cover is mostly bigleaf maple and Douglas-fir. After a hefty bit of climbing and another mile of trail, a small spur trail forks right to a viewpoint of the Gorge and opposing mountains. This is a good place for a break and some water.

Next, the trail flattens out slightly through more firs and some western red cedar trees. You will notice many downed trees. Some are still lying across the trail, waiting for the saw, while others decompose into the soil nearby. Wind, wet soil around the roots, heavy snow on branches, and disease all contribute to fallen wood. This natural thinning of the forest reduces fire danger and facilitates the survival of the largest and strongest trees.

Soon the trail starts climbing again, becoming steeper and steeper as it passes through smaller and smaller trees. At almost 4 miles up, the trail

*Mount Defiance from Dog Mountain Trail.*

enters the Columbia Wilderness; the border is marked only by a permit box. Fill out your free permit and keep climbing.

Because of the elevation, the forest now consists mostly of lodgepole and whitebark pines and subalpine firs. Then the trail breaks out onto a massive tallus slope, from which you will catch your first view of the microwave tower on top of Mount Defiance. Seeing the summit will give you a second wind. Continue along the open slope, bearing left, to the junction with Mitchell Point Trail 417 to Warren Lake. Stay right for Mount Defiance.

About 0.2 mile farther you'll reach an unmarked junction. Either trail can take you to the top, but the left trail goes straight up whereas the right trail runs gently around the mountain to the other side for a short backtrack up to the top. If you are returning via the same trail, straight is quickest. If you are continuing on to the Bear Lake or North Lake area, stay right.

The trail passes through the tallus slope, seen from below, and curves into dense subalpine forest. Then the trail winds upward toward the west, onto another tallus slope, before leaving the Columbia Wilderness. Below and to the west, Bear Lake is visible, surrounded by forested slopes in an old glacial cirque. The same glaciers also sculpted the volcanic rock of Mount Defiance into a steep point. After leaving the Columbia Wilderness, cross another tallus slope to the junction. Turn left for the summit, right for North Lake. The 0.2 mile to the summit passes through subalpine fir trees stunted by wind and cold. The summit offers incredible views in all directions.

# MOUNT DEFIANCE AND STARVATION RIDGE TRAIL

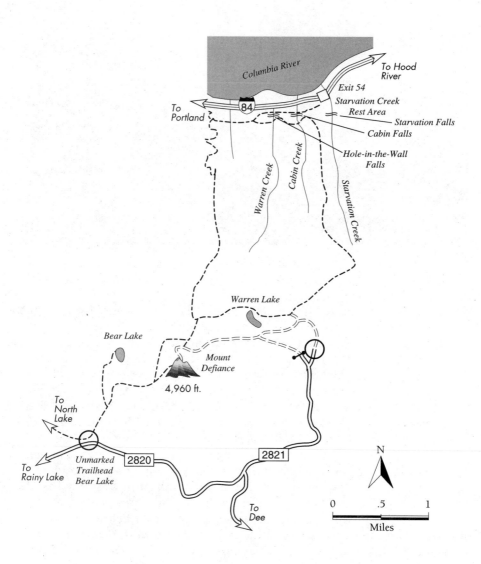

Columbia River

To Hood River

Exit 54

Starvation Creek Rest Area

Starvation Falls

Cabin Falls

Hole-in-the-Wall Falls

To Portland

84

Warren Creek

Cabin Creek

Starvation Creek

Warren Lake

Bear Lake

Mount Defiance

4,960 ft.

To North Lake

To Rainy Lake

Unmarked Trailhead Bear Lake

2820

2821

To Dee

N

0    .5    1
Miles

The radio facility at the top, and the roads nearby, make this achievement not as unique as you might like it after the challenging climb from the gorge, but it is spectacular and not everybody can say they climbed Mount Defiance the "real" way.

Return via the same route.

## BEAR LAKE OPTION:

You can access this area from the Bear Lake Trailhead or leave a car there for a point-to-point hike. From the junction with the Mount Defiance Trail 413 and the trail running around Mount Defiance, the path descends steadily for 0.9 mile to the junction with Bear Lake Trail 413B. The junction is marked by a large pile of rocks, somewhat like a cairn, but not obvious. Turn right, heading north for Bear Lake, and gently descend through lodgepole pines to the lake. It's surrounded by trees, but offers good views of the mountain above. There are at least two sites and room for multiple tents, plus a fire pit and fishing opportunities.

## NORTH LAKE OPTION:

To make an even larger loop, you can leave a car at the Wyeth Trailhead and continue past the junction with Bear Lake. The trail levels out before a cut area through the trees, to the left, signals the wilderness boundary and the intersection with Forest Road 2820 and Wyeth Trail 411.

Turn right on Wyeth Trail 411 for North Lake. The trail is mostly level, with slight ups and downs through middle-aged hemlock forest for 0.7 mile to the junction with the Rainy/North Lake Trail and the Wyeth Trail 411. Turn left, and 100 yards later turn right for North Lake.

North Lake offers views of Green Point and good campsites on both ends of the lake. It is not that far from the Rainy Lake Campground and receives relatively heavy use. North Lake is rumored to have fish, but it was raining so hard when I got there that I didn't feel much like fishing. North Lake is not that far from Rainy Lake and not that different in atmospheric persuasion.

From North Lake, follow Wyeth Trail 411 as described in the Wyeth Trail to North Lake Hike.

# 35  STARVATION RIDGE TRAIL

See Map on Page 124

| | |
|---|---|
| **General description:** | A very strenuous hike to Warren Lake and Mount Defiance, with some loop options. |
| **Distance:** | 5.6 miles. |
| **Difficulty:** | Difficult. |
| **Traffic:** | Light. |
| **Trail type:** | Maintained. |
| **Best season:** | April through October. |
| **Elevation gain:** | 3,640 feet. |
| **Maximum elevation:** | 3,800 feet. |
| **Topographic maps:** | Mount Defiance USGS and Hood River Green Trails. |

**Finding the trailhead:** From Portland, take Interstate 84 east to the Starvation Creek Rest Area, just after Wyeth Exit 51, heading east. If you get to Viento State Park, you have gone too far. The rest area is accessible only from the eastbound side. Mount Defiance Trail 413 starts on the right, just to the west, before the parking lot. Bathrooms are available at the trailhead.

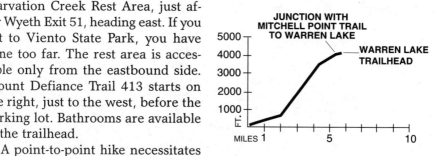

A point-to-point hike necessitates a shuttle from the Warren Lake trailhead. Drive east to Hood River Exit 62 and turn right, following the signs to the city center on Oak. At the 13th Street stoplight turn right, heading south along the main route. Stay left on Tucker Road, following the signs to Dee. At Dee, turn right onto Lost Lake Road, cross some railroad tracks, and turn right onto Punch Bowl Road. Green Road veers left 0.2 mile later but stay right, heading north. After 1 mile turn left onto Dead Point Road, heading west up Dead Point Creek on Forest Road 2820. At 7.5 miles is FR 620; stay left on Forest Road 2820. At 9.4 miles is the junction with FR 2821; stay right, heading east. At 9.8 miles the road is blocked by a gate. Another road to the right is blocked by a dirt pile.

## Key points:
|      |                                                      |
|------|------------------------------------------------------|
| 0.3  | Junction with Starvation Ridge Cutoff Trail 414A     |
| 1.0  | Junction with Starvation Ridge Trail 414             |
| 2.0  | Junction with rejoining Starvation Ridge Cutoff Trail 414A |
| 4.3  | Junction with Viento Ridge Spur Trail 417            |
| 5.3  | Junction with Mitchell Point trail 417 to Warren Lake |
| 5.6  | Warren Lake Trailhead                                |

*Looking west from Starvation Ridge Trail.*

**The trail:** The Starvation Ridge Trail is not easy. It climbs over 3,000 feet in less than 4 miles. The trail does not switchback much and climbs straight up the ridge. The Starvation Ridge Trail is not as well known as the Mount Defiance Trail but is in my opinion the toughest hike in the Columbia Gorge, especially with a pack. This is a very strenuous day hike, but makes a good overnight trip for athletes and climbers trying to get in shape. After climbing to Warren Lake you probably won't want to leave it right away anyway, so stay a night. Warren Lake has brook trout and good camping, despite heavy use.

The Starvation Creek Rest Area has a short nature path to the bottom of Starvation Falls. Both the ridge and the falls are named after the 1884-1885, three-week plight of stranded railroad passengers. Starvation Falls is worth a look. A water fountain nearby is a good place to fill water bottles. The climb up Starvation Ridge requires a lot of sweat and does not provide water after Cabin Creek.

Start on Mount Defiance Trail 413, which begins at the west end of the rest area. The path runs parallel to Interstate 84 for 0.3 mile to the junction with Starvation Ridge Cutoff Trail 414A. The fork left is the most direct route to the Starvation Ridge Trail. It immediately switchbacks up for 0.5 mile before rejoining the main Starvation Ridge Trail. You will get plenty of steep climbing, so it might be a good idea to follow the Defiance Trail 413 and take the more gradual scenic route up Starvation Ridge Trail 414 just after the Warren Creek crossing. This allows for a short warm-up.

Stay right, heading west on the Mount Defiance Trail 413, which passes Cabin Falls; the falls is not easily seen from the trail. Continue straight on the Mount Defiance Trail to a footbridge just below Hole-in-the-Wall Falls. These falls are manmade, created after the construction of the original Columbia Gorge Highway.

A short mile beyond Warren Creek you'll reach the junction with the Starvation Ridge Trail to Warren Lake. Turn left and climb gradually around the ridge to Warren Creek, which you must ford. The trail switchbacks up onto a steep grassy meadow, rich in wildflowers and skirted by Oregon oak. The powerlines above distract slightly from the view, but the familiar profiles of Dog and Wind mountains are easily seen across the gorge.

After leaving the meadow behind, round the second ridge and cross Cabin Creek in the trees. This is your last place for water until Warren Lake, which is 4 miles further uphill. At 2 miles, Starvation Cutoff Trail 414A rejoins the main trail. Once you hit this junction I hope you are warmed up, because it is all uphill from here. This trail deserves respect, and if you don't respect it now, you will in a couple of miles.

From the junction, the trail climbs steeply on switchbacks until cresting the ridge for more views west, down the Gorge. After the trail crests the ridge, the nice switchbacks end and the ridgetop crawl begins. There is only about one place along the way to get a view. Try to focus on the increasing sense of peace as you get higher and higher, away from the highway, the smell of pine, the vision of an alpine lake, and the healthy heart.

After 2.3 miles of straight-up climbing from the Starvation Ridge Cutoff junction, the trail veers to the right as an old trail to Viento Ridge veers left. At this point, most of the steep climbing is done; the remaining trail to Warren Lake follows a gentle uphill grade. The view in this area is subject to human intervention and the abundance of tree harvesting. After turning right, continue to keep right as an old road forks left, and enjoy another viewpoint before passing through another logged area by the junction with Mitchell Point Trail 417. Stay right and fill out your wilderness permit at the end of the logged area. You are now entering the Columbia Wilderness.

Warren Lake is 0.3 mile further, and has several good campsites with well-used fire rings. Above Warren Lake are several tallus slopes which give the lake an alpine feel and a beautiful panoramic setting, especially if you wade out to catch a fish.

After climbing this trail you may need someone to pick you up, take you home and put you to bed. I can't guarantee that Mom will meet you at Forest Road 2821, but you might want to make vehicle arrangements anyway. From the junction with Mitchell Point Trail to Warren Lake, head south on Trail 417A for the 0.25 mile to the car.

Otherwise, return to the trailhead via the same route.

---

## MOUNT DEFIANCE TRAIL LOOP OPTION:

After resting a night at Warren Lake, climb west on the Mitchell Point Trail to the Mount Defiance Trail. Go left and south the rest of the way up the mountain; right takes you back to the Starvation Creek Rest Area on a grade similar to the one you climbed up. See the Mount Defiance Hike for more details.

# 36  WYGANT TRAIL AND PERHAM CREEK LOOP

| | |
|---|---|
| **General description:** | A steep day hike up Wygant Point, with shorter scenic options along Perham Creek. |
| **Distance:** | 8 miles. |
| **Difficulty:** | Difficult to top of mountain. Easy to Moderate for loop. |
| **Traffic:** | Light. |
| **Trail Type:** | Maintained. |
| **Best season:** | Year-round, depending on frost line. |
| **Elevation gain:** | 2,050 feet. |
| **Maximum elevation:** | 2,214 feet. |
| **Topographic maps:** | Hood River, Mount Defiance USGS and Hood River Green Trails. |

**Finding the trailhead:** From Portland, take Interstate 84 east to Mitchell Point, about 3 miles before the first Hood River exit. Follow the off-ramp up to the Mitchell Point parking lot. The Wygant Trail starts at a gated jeep trail on the right, to the west, just before the parking lot. Bathrooms are available at the trailhead.

**Note: The trailhead is only accessible from eastbound Interstate 84.**

**Key points:**
- 0.2   Junction with jeep trail
- 0.7   Junction with Wygant Trail, old highway ends
- 1.0   Junction with Perham Loop Trail
- 2.5   Junction with Chetwoot Trail back to Perham Creek
- 4.0   Top of Wygant Point

**The trail:** The Wygant Trail is one of the lesser known gorge trails, but it has some spectacular views. Wygant Point is quiet and pristine, but getting to it is not easy. A hike to the top is 8 miles, round trip. The Perham Creek Loop option (5 miles round trip) offers an easier hike, with rushing streams and cool cedar trees.

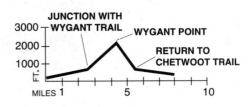

The trail begins at the gate at Mitchell Point, along an abandoned stretch of the old Gorge Highway, which parallels the interstate for 0.25 mile. Then,

# WYGANT POINT

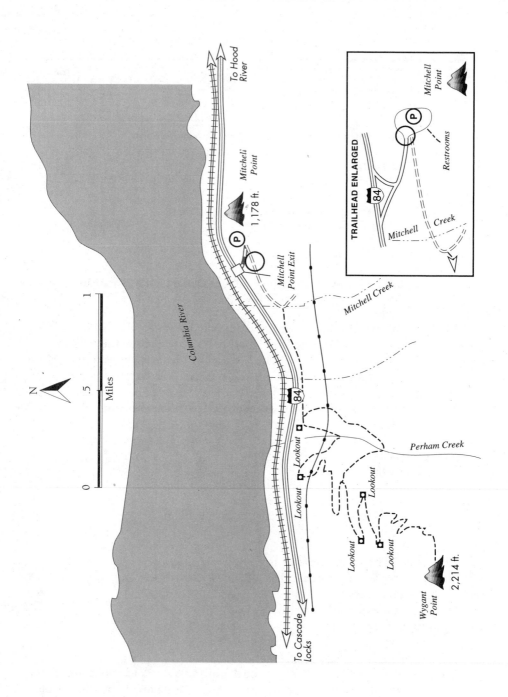

N

Miles

0     .5     1

Columbia River

To Hood River

Mitchell Point
1,178 ft.

P

Mitchell Point Exit

Mitchell Creek

84

Lookout

Lookout

Perham Creek

Lookout

Lookout

Lookout

Wygant Point
2,214 ft.

To Cascade Locks

**TRAILHEAD ENLARGED**

Mitchell Point

P

Restrooms

84

Mitchell Creek

after a small clearing, a jeep trail curves uphill to the left while the Wygant Trail forks right. Next, the trail crosses seasonally-wet Mitchell Creek. There is no footbridge, so a spring ford will mean wet feet. Soon after crossing Mitchell Creek, the trail rejoins the overgrown highway.

At 0.7 mile the trail forks left, leaving the old highway, which disappears in the direction of Interstate 84. Remnants of a small landslide caused by flooding in 1996 are visible above the junction. The faint trail follows the scoured creekbed. In several places the trail is washed out, and scrambling up to the next switchback is necessary. The trail climbs steeply out of the gully, and two short switchbacks later levels out. It passes several old Douglas-fir trees and younger, moss-covered Oregon oaks.

At 1 mile, Perham Loop Trail joins the Wygant Trail from the south (left). This trail up to the Perham Creek Loop climbs steadily, until dropping down to cross Perham Creek. It rejoins the Wygant Trail in another 1.5 miles. It is better for the return trip, so stay right, continuing west.

This trail proceeds 50 feet to a T junction. The right fork, to the north, is a spur trail to a viewpoint. Stay left, continuing west, as the Wygant Trail descends into the Perham Creek Valley. The floods of 1996 destroyed the old log footbridge that used to cross this creek. You can follow the remaining pieces of the old bridge part of the way across, but at some point it will be necessary to get your feet wet. Be careful: it is difficult to negotiate the fallen debris. The trail is not immediately apparent on the other side, but look upstream, to the south. About 100 yards upstream from the old bridge you'll see the trail next to a large fir.

After Perham Creek the trail climbs up onto a shelf. It levels out for the 1.7 miles to the Columbia River Lookout. This offers prime views of Cook Hill directly across the river and Dog Mountain just to the west. This is a good spot to spy on the anglers below. In the spring, look for early blue violets on this grassy point. After the Columbia River Lookout, the trail passes underneath some powerlines and begins to switchback upward.

At 2.5 miles, the Chetwoot Trail forks left for the continuation of the Perham Loop, heading east.

---

### WYGANT POINT OPTION:

The right fork leads directly to Wygant Point. The switchbacks continue. At the west elbow of several of the switchbacks, spur trails climb out onto steep clifftop views. These views can distract you from the burning muscles of rapid climbing. You may find that this hill suffers from a little bit of the never-ending switchback disease. Just when you think, this is the last switchback...there's another one. Try to focus on the temperate forest that surrounds you. Along the way many of the trees are very old, and the trail is quiet and shady. The forest floor is home to common sword ferns and Cascade Oregon grape.

The upper reaches of this trail offer even greater isolation. Just before the crest, Wygant State Park comes to an end and the Mount Hood National Forest begins. At the marked boundary, the Perham Creek drainage is visible below to the south. The summit is a modest pile of rocks, surrounded by a stand of young firs. It is quiet enough to scare up a grouse or two.

On the way back, take the right fork, heading east, on the Chetwoot Trail that connects with the Perham Loop. The trail descends and traverses the contours of Wygant Ridge into a cooler, wetter environment of western red cedar. As noted earlier, this crossing of Perham Creek is also bridgeless. Getting your feet wet might be better than slipping on exposed rocks in an attempt to hop across.

 When fording a stream, small rocks are generally more stable and provide better traction than large, slippery rocks.

On the opposite side, the trail climbs for a short while, then descends gradually, crossing underneath the powerlines again to a jeep trail. Follow the jeep trail right for 50 feet before turning north and down on the Perham Loop. Soon after, the trail rejoins the main Wygant Trail for the last mile back to the trailhead.


# GOV. TOM MᶜCALL PRESERVE

**Overview:**

The Tom McCall Preserve is a combination of state land in Mayer State Park, national forest, and private land owned by The Nature Conservancy (TNC), a private non-profit organization, which manages the area without state funding. Because thousands of people visit each year, TNC asks that you follow several use guidelines designed to preserve the natural heritage of the area. It is a great place for bird-watching. A "stay-on-the-trail" ethic on the part of visitors keeps the landscape pristine despite heavy visitation. The preserve is famous for its wildflowers, especially the radiant purple Columbia desert parsley. There is no drinking water or restrooms on the preserve.

**Use Guidelines:**

1. Stay on trails.
2. Do not disturb vegetation, wildlife, or scientific study plots.
3. No dogs or horses, which disturb ground-nesting birds and other wildlife.
4. No mountain bikes.
5. No hunting or firearms.
6. No camping or fires.

7. Do not litter.
8. The trail to McCall Point is closed from October through April, because of resource damage concerns.
9. Watch out for poison oak, ticks, and rattlesnakes.

# 37   ROWENA PLATEAU

| | |
|---|---|
| **General description:** | A gentle nature walk on Mayer State Park, USDA Forest Service, and Nature Conservancy land famous for wildflowers. |
| **Distance:** | 2.4 miles. |
| **Difficulty:** | Easy. |
| **Traffic:** | Heavy. |
| **Trail Type:** | Maintained. |
| **Best season:** | March through June for wildflowers. |
| **Elevation gain:** | -400 feet. |
| **Maximum elevation:** | 700 feet. |
| **Topographic maps:** | Lyle USGS. |

**Finding the trailhead:** From Portland, take Interstate 84 east to Exit 69 at Mosier. Turn right on Highway 30, heading east on the Historic Columbia River Highway. Drive 6.5 miles. The trailhead is on the left, opposite the loop road to Rowena Crest Viewpoint.

**Key points:**
    0.3    Junction with top loop around Vernal Pond
    0.8    Second Vernal Pond
    1.2    Spur trail to a lookout over the Gorge

**The trail:** The hike out onto the Rowena Plateau is not much of a work-out at 2.4 miles. This is a better hike for those who are in a nature-loving mood. Rowena Plateau offers a diverse group of wildflowers, from balsamroot and Columbia desert parsley to monkeyflowers, buttercups, and broad-leafed lupine.

At the trailhead, there is a sign-in board that helps TNC monitor the number of people who visit the preserve. Please sign in and look over the information provided about the preserve by TNC. The interpretive display provides a preview of the flora and fauna commonly seen at Tom McCall.

 It is a good idea to carry your favorite flower or bird book on this walk. You are guaranteed plenty of chances to use it.

From the trailhead, the grade is level to slightly downhill, following a

# ROWENA PLATEAU AND MCCALL POINT

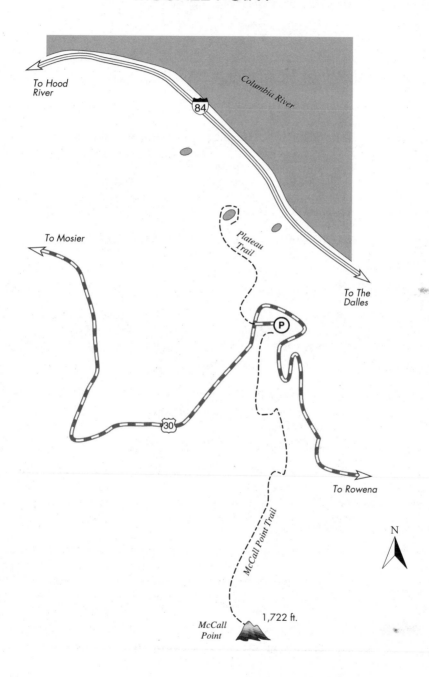

To Hood River

Columbia River

84

To Mosier

Plateau Trail

To The Dalles

P

30

To Rowena

McCall Point Trail

N

McCall Point

1,722 ft.

singletrack people path. Soon the trail curves right, toward the gorge, and then left through an old stone fence from the days when this plateau was grazed. The plateau has cliffs on all sides except this entrance, and only a small fence was needed to contain cattle. The aftermath of this, however, is that there is not as much balsamroot on this plateau, because cows like the big, soft leaves. The area has not been grazed recently, but balsamroot is still sparse past the stone fence. TNC is working to restore some of the native plant populations on several portions of the plateau.

At 0.3 mile is the junction with the top loop around one of two vernal ponds. Going right at the unmarked junction takes you around the pond for a view of Lyle and the Klickitat Valley beyond. Left continues down the plateau.

Heading west, there is a side trail down to the pond for a bird-watching stop. Shortly after the loop trail rejoins the main trail, continue left further out onto Rowena Plateau. The scenery is much the same, with fields of flowers and grasses and Oregon oak in the surrounding ponds. This can be dull if you don't like the little things, or it can be exhilarating to look for the smallest flower and listen for the slightest variation in the songs of the birds.

At the second vernal pond there is another side trail down to the edge, but this trail is skirted by poison oak. The understory, aside from poison oak, is composed primarily of snowberrry and serviceberry. You can also tell that this preserve is dryer than many of the places west in the gorge, because of the absence of moss on the oak trees.

Continue on down the plateau through the open mound and swale topography to a lookout. A spur trail forks right on top of the basalt cliffs of the gorge. You might feel a little of the updrafts from below that could lift your wings, if you had any.

Continuing down the trail offers much of the same, with more areas for plant exploration and identification. The return trip is slightly uphill along the same trail.

See Map on Page 134

| | |
|---|---|
| **General Description:** | A gentle ascent up McCall Point. |
| **Distance:** | 3.0 miles. |
| **Difficulty:** | Moderate to top. |
| **Trail type:** | Well-maintained. |
| **Traffic:** | Moderate to heavy. |
| **Best season:** | May through September; closed October through April. |
| **Elevation gain:** | 1,100 feet. |
| **Maximum elevation:** | 1,700 feet. |
| **Topographic maps:** | Lyle USGS. |

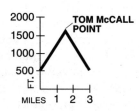

**Finding the trailhead:** From Portland, take Interstate 84 east to Exit 69 at Mosier. Turn right on Highway 30 and head east on the Columbia Gorge Scenic Highway. Drive 6.5 miles and turn right onto a loop road to Rowena Crest. The trailhead is just to the right of the paved turnaround; this is the best place to park.

**Key points:**
- 0.7   Junction with deadend trail at Nature Conservancy sign
- 1.5   Top of  McCall Point

**The trail:** The trail to the top of McCall Point is not strenuous, but neither is it easy. The trail offers many views due to only a sparse covering of Oregon oaks and ponderosa pines. From the top, on a clear day, the view of Mount Hood is spectacular. The area receives heavy, but surprisingly polite foot traffic. Off-trail habitat is preserved remarkably well and offers places for many species of birds, flowers, and other wildlife. One of these species is the rattlesnake: beautiful but dangerous.

   In rattlesnake country, it is best to stay on the trail. Rattlesnakes generally avoid areas of heavy human traffic, and are most common on the rocky slopes away from the trail.

The trail starts along the grassy scab land left by the ancient Missoula floods. The trail follows  along an old road, which is level, and winds toward the forested hillside above. Several large ponderosa pines sculpted by the wind offer resting spots for the common birds of the area. Kestrels and red-tailed hawks are commonly seen on the preserve. As the trail enters the more forested area, watch out for poison oak along the side of the old road. This is also a good place to see Columbia desert parsley with its bright purple flowers and pillowy green leaves. The trail rounds the edge of the

*Lyle from McCall Point Trail.*

hillside and traverses along the east slope until reaching a marked junction. This is the where the main trail forks right off of the old road. The old road keeps heading straight for a while.

The trail continues to climb through moss-covered oaks and snowberry plants. In the spring, you can sometimes catch a glacier lily in bloom along the way. Next, switchbacks follow the ridge up, with views of the Gorge below and to the east.

There's about 0.5 mile of switchbacks to reach the summit. From the top, on a clear day, you can get a good view of Mount Hood and Mount Adams. A faint trail continues further, but is on private land; please respect this boundary. The summit of McCall Point is a great place to have lunch and enjoy the surrounding vista before returning via the same trail. Please choose your lunch spot to minimize impact on the vegetation

| | |
|---|---|
| **General Description:** | A wheelchair-accessible nature trail along the Columbia River outside of Skamania. |
| **Distance:** | 0.5 mile. |
| **Difficulty:** | Easy. |
| **Traffic:** | Moderate. |
| **Trail type:** | Maintained trail. |
| **Best season:** | Year-round. |
| **Elevation gain:** | 0 feet. |
| **Maximum elevation:** | 60 feet. |
| **Topographic maps:** | No map shows this trail. |

**Finding the trailhead:** From Vancouver, take Washington State Highway 41 east for 11 miles to Milepost 30 and turn right 0.1 mile later, heading south. Saint Cloud Recreation Area is across the tracks. Parking and bathrooms are available at the trailhead.

## SAINT CLOUD NATURE TRAIL

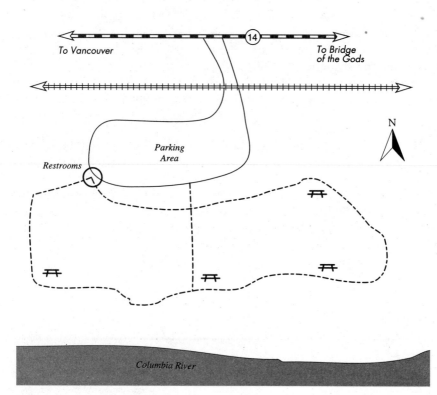

**The trail:** This area is a brand new nature trail for the Columbia River Gorge National Scenic Area. You can picnic, walk, and possibly see an osprey; one nests on the far side of the river on a channel marker, allowing it to fly by this side looking for food. The area is named for the Saint Cloud Ranch, which was a vacation home for the Vials. Originally, Paul and Florence Vial named their beloved home the Saint Cloud Ranch after the suburb of Paris where they honeymooned in 1903. The ranch was their summer home.

The trail begins at the west end of the parking lot and makes a large counter-clockwise loop through some apple trees and along the Columbia River. The old apple orchard has been reclaimed by nature, but some of the Newton Pippon apple trees still remain. The section along the river is a wild, undeveloped beach and marsh area, perfect for wildlife. The area suffers from the common invasive species of Himalayan blackberry, but otherwise is a comfortable place to stroll by the river.

## 40  SAMS-WALKER NATURE TRAIL

| | |
|---|---|
| **General Description:** | A wheelchair-accessible nature trail along the Columbia River outside of Skamania. |
| **Distance:** | 1.7 miles. |
| **Difficulty:** | Easy. |
| **Traffic:** | Moderate. |
| **Trail type:** | Maintained trail. |
| **Best season:** | Year-round. |
| **Elevation gain:** | 0 feet. |
| **Maximum elevation:** | 60 feet. |
| **Topographic maps:** | No map shows this trail. |

**Finding the trailhead:** From Vancouver, take Washington State Highway 41 east for 11 miles to Milepost 30 and turn right 0.8 mile later, heading south. Sams-Walker Recreation Area is across the tracks. Parking and bathrooms are available at the trailhead.

**The trail:** This area is a brand new nature trail for the Columbia Gorge National Scenic Area. You can picnic, walk, and enjoy the possibility of seeing wildlife.

The site is an integral part of Skamania County history and is dedicated to the Sams and Walker families who owned the site from 1903 to 1969. Before them, Watlala Indians occupied the shoreline because of the plentiful fish harvests.

The trail starts at the south end of the parking lot and joins a large loop trail running along the Columbia River. There are several places to take

# SAMS-WALKER NATURE TRAIL

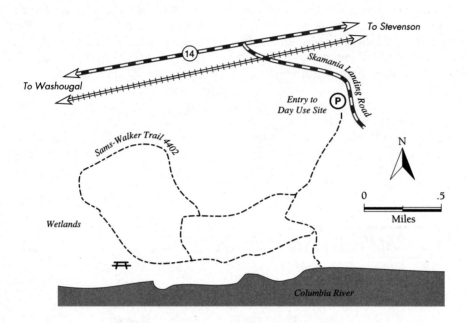

pictures, and some picnic tables. The seasonal wetlands support forests of Oregon oak and black cottonwood. The section along the river is a wild, undeveloped beach and marsh area, perfect for wildlife.

# BEACON ROCK STATE PARK

**Overview:**

Beacon Rock marks the place where Lewis & Clark first noticed the rise and fall of the tides. They then knew they were finally on the last leg of their journey to the Pacific.

The Hamilton Mountain Trail offers both easy and difficult day hiking. It is an easy 1.4-mile hike to Rodney and Hardy falls. It is 4 miles to the summit of Hamilton Mountain, and past the falls it is almost all uphill. Beacon Rock State Park was established in 1935. This area is one of the premier hiking areas on the Washington side of the Gorge, and has a well-maintained trail.

## 41   BEACON ROCK

| | |
|---|---|
| **General description:** | A short, steep day hike to the top of Beacon Rock . |
| **Distance:** | 2.2 miles. |
| **Difficulty:** | Moderate. |
| **Traffic:** | Heavy. |
| **Trail type:** | Guardrail-protected path. |
| **Best season:** | Year-round, depending on frost line. |
| **Elevation gain:** | 600 feet. |
| **Maximum elevation:** | 850 feet. |
| **Topographic maps:** | Bridal Veil USGS. |

**Finding the trailhead:** From Portland, take Interstate 84 east to Cascade Locks. Cross the Columbia River on the Bridge of the Gods for a toll of 75 cents. Turn left, heading west, on Washington State Highway 14 for 7 miles. Two parking lots for Beacon Rock State Park are available on the left, south side. The trailhead is at the west end of the first parking lot. Public restrooms are at the east end of the first parking lot.

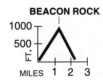

**Key points:**
1.1    Top of Beacon Rock

**The trail:** The heavily traveled trail to the top of Beacon Rock is paved in some places, boardwalked in others, and surrounded by a safety guardrail most of the way up. It is not so much a wilderness experience as an urban park. The view is spectacular, and the location deeply historical.

You will probably see many kids and families; however, I do not recom-

# BEACON ROCK

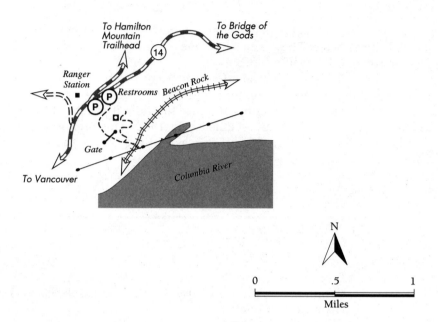

mend this trail for children because it hikes up a cliff and the guardrail is a single pipe, offering insufficient protection for. I recommend instead the Rodney and Hardy Falls Hike.

The trail climbs around the west side of Beacon Rock to a steel-gated enclosure on the cliff. The enclosure consists of a large metal plate with a door cut into it, and it's surrounded by razor wire. To get around this obstacle when the trail is closed would be practically impossible.

Past the metal gate the trail climbs switchbacks upward. Wooden planks hold you up as you proceed along the cliff, with views of the Gorge and Munra Point across the river. Upriver there is a good view of Bonneville Dam and the Cascade Locks. This trail proves that engineers can build a trail anywhere they want to.

Further up, the trail enters a fir stand atop the rock and climbs to the final lookout. From this vantage point there are good views of Hamilton Mountain and Table Mountain to the northeast.

| | |
|---|---|
| **General description:** | A gentle day hike to Hardy and Rodney falls. |
| **Distance:** | 2.8 miles |
| **Difficulty:** | Easy. |
| **Traffic:** | Moderate to heavy. |
| **Trail type:** | Well-maintained. |
| **Best season:** | Year-round, depending on frost line. |
| **Elevation gain:** | 600 feet. |
| **Maximum elevation:** | 1,000 feet. |
| **Topographic maps:** | Beacon Rock USGS and Bridal Veil Green Trails. |

**Finding the trailhead:** From Portland, take Interstate 84 east to Cascade Locks. Cross the Columbia River on the Bridge of the Gods for a toll of 75 cents. Turn left and head west on Washington State Highway 14 for 7 miles. Turn right at Beacon Rock State Park, just opposite Beacon Rock. Follow the park road for 0.25 mile to the first picnic area on the right. The trailhead is at the east end of the parking lot, behind the public restrooms.

**Key points:**
  0.5  Junction with campground trail
  1.3  Junction with spur trail down to Hardy Falls overlook
  1.4  Junction with Pool of the Winds spur trail to Rodney Falls

**The trail:** Instead of climbing Hamilton Mountain, one can opt for the less strenuous hike to Rodney and Hardy falls. The trail is graded gently uphill and is a better choice for children than the Beacon Rock hike. There aren't very many waterfalls on the Washington side of the Columbia River Gorge, but these are two of the gems.

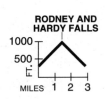

From the picnic area, the trail climbs gradually through large Douglas-firs and a mix of smaller, deciduous trees. At 0.5 mile, the trail intersects with the campground trail, just underneath the powerlines. One disadvantage of the Washington side of the gorge is that almost all of the hiking trails must pass beneath these powerlines, whereas many of the Multnomah Falls area hikes on the Oregon side do not. Stay right, continuing northeast, for the falls.

At 1.3 miles is a spur trail to the Hardy Falls overlook. The right, unmarked fork, on the south side of the trail, descends downhill for 200 yards to a circular set of benches above Hardy Creek. Hardy Falls is just barely visible from this overlook.

# RODNEY AND HARDY FALLS AND HAMILTON MOUNTAIN

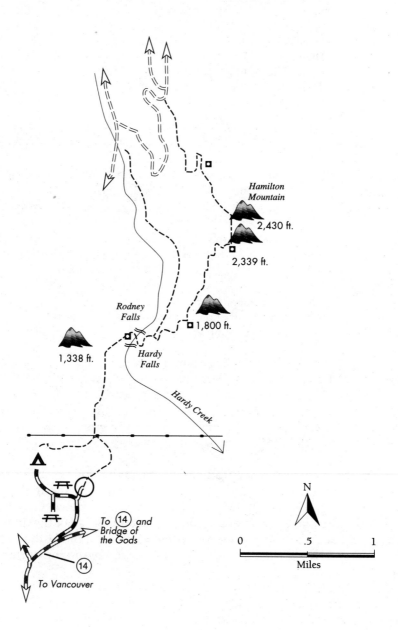

Hamilton
Mountain

2,430 ft.

2,339 ft.

Rodney
Falls

1,800 ft.

1,338 ft.

Hardy
Falls

Hardy Creek

To (14) and
Bridge of
the Gods

(14)

To Vancouver

N

0          .5          1
Miles

At 1.4 miles, another spur trail forks left, on the northeast side of the trail, to the Pool of the Winds and Rodney Falls. Pool of the Winds is a deep bowl carved out of the rock by Rodney Falls, which has just a small vertical slit in the rock for an outlet. The short spur trail climbs up to the area just outside the pool. A guardrail prevents hikers from falling on the slick rock, and a log bench offers weary hikers a cool resting spot. It is necessary to follow the guardrail all the way to the end in order to see inside the bowl. Don't be surprised if you get a cool blast of mist on your face. The mist is responsible for the slick rock, and despite the guardrail caution is warranted.

Return via the same route to the trailhead, or continue on to Hamilton Mountain (Hike 43).

# 43  HAMILTON MOUNTAIN

| | |
|---|---|
| **General description:** | A steep day hike to the top of Hamilton Mountain, passing Hardy and Rodney Falls. |
| **Distance:** | 9 miles. |
| **Difficulty:** | Difficult. |
| **Traffic:** | Moderate to heavy. |
| **Trail type:** | Well-maintained. |
| **Best season:** | Year-round, depending on frost line. |
| **Elevation gain:** | 2,017 feet. |
| **Maximum elevation:** | 2,445 feet. |
| **Topographic maps:** | Bridal Veil USGS and Bridal Veil Green Trails. |

**Finding the trailhead:** From Portland, take Interstate 84 east to Cascade Locks. Cross the Columbia River on the Bridge of the Gods for a toll of 75 cents. Turn left, heading west, on Washington State Highway 14 for 7 miles. Turn right at Beacon Rock State Park, just opposite Beacon Rock. Follow the park road for 0.25 mile to the first picnic area on the right. The trailhead is at the far end of the parking lot, behind the public restrooms.

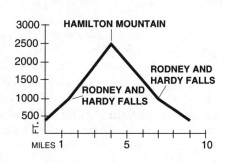

**Key points:**
>    0.5   Junction with campground trail
>    1.3   Junction with spur trail down to Hardy Falls overlook.
>    1.4   Junction with Pool of the Winds spur trail to Rodney Falls
>    1.8   Junction with loop trail from Hamilton Ridge
>    4.0   Top of Hamilton Mountain

**The trail:** The Hamilton Mountain Trail climbs 4 miles to the top of Hamilton Mountain, and once past the falls it is almost all uphill. This portion of Beacon Rock State Park offers spectacular views, but some sections of the trail are very steep and you should consider carefully before taking the southern route to the top. There is a less treacherous route, described as the return route for this hike, that runs to the north after Rodney Falls.

From the picnic area the trail climbs gradually until it intersects the campground trail at 0.5 mile. Stay right, heading north and east for Hamilton Mountain. At 1.3 miles is a spur trail to the Hardy Falls overlook, from which the falls are just barely visible. After visiting the falls continue northeast, bearing left, on the main trail.

At 1.4 miles, another spur trail forks left, northeast, to the Pool of the Winds and Rodney Falls. Pool of the Winds is a deep bowl carved out of the rock by Rodney Falls. You can follow a guardrailed path all the way to the end of the spur trail for a look into the Pool of the Winds. The rocks are slick, so be careful.

Next, continue on the Hamilton Mountain trail. The trail descends on weathered switchbacks and crosses Hardy Creek on a footbridge. Then you begin climbing steep switchbacks.

At 1.8 miles is an unmarked fork. The left trail, to the north, goes up the Hardy Creek drainage. It is a longer, more gradual route to the top. The right trail, to the east, is a continuation of the Hamilton Mountain Trail. It climbs steeply, often close to the edge, with the Gorge visible below. If you don't like being on the edge, take the left fork. The right trail is better for people impatient to get to the top and who don't mind steep switchbacks. The left trail is for people who like to take a somewhat longer but less crowded route. The elevation gain is the same for both routes, but the left route up the Hardy Creek drainage is a mile longer. If you take the left fork, follow the description of the upper loop in reverse.

The right fork, to the east, keeps climbing after the junction. After about a mile of switchbacks the trail levels off a bit. It follows the ridge before reverting to switchbacks for the final ascent. The summit of Hamilton Mountain is covered by brush, so the views along the way are better. Table Mountain, Mount Hood, and Nesmith Point are all visible on a clear day. Take a rest while deciding which way to go down. I recommend the ridge trail that continues left beyond the summit. Better views await you down the ridge.

The loop trail continues along the ridge, dropping down several switchbacks, and opens up into a lava field. The lava field is great place to spend a few contemplative moments; the views here are superior to those from the summit. Mount St. Helens is sometimes visible in the distance, adding to the Gorge panorama. At the other end of the lava clearing, there are three choices of trail/logging roads. Take the left one, heading west, to complete the loop.

This logging road descends 1 mile into the Hardy Creek drainage. There are some huge stumps here and there among the trees of a young deciduous and fir forest. Most of these stumps have burn marks, and the unattached snag is usually decomposing somewhere nearby. These clues indicate a burn rather than a harvest.

Just before reaching a clearing, a logging road forks right up the drainage. Stay left, heading south and west, on the loop. At the clearing the logging road crosses over Hardy Creek, to the west. The loop trail forks left, continuing south, before crossing the creek on a small catwalk. Just remember to keep left. The loop trail continues another 1.2 miles to rejoin the Hamilton Mountain Trail. Turn right for the last 1.8 miles back to the trailhead.

Consider the campground trail for variety on the return route. It follows the powerlines, then drops through "Hadley's Grove," marked by a petrified stump dedicated to the first superintendent of Beacon Rock State Park, Clyde B. Hadley. His grove is actually a young stand of fir, much smaller than the ancient trees in the campground just a little further on. The trail terminates at the upper end of the campground loop. From the campground it is a short walk down the paved road to the picnic area.

# 44   GILLETTE LAKE

| | |
|---|---|
| **General description:** | A 5-mile round-trip day hike to Gillette Lake on the famous Pacific Crest Trail (PCT). |
| **Distance:** | 5 miles. |
| **Difficulty:** | Easy to Gillette Lake, strenuous to Table Mountain. |
| **Traffic:** | Moderate. |
| **Trail type:** | Well-maintained. |
| **Best season:** | Year-round |
| **Elevation gain:** | 280 feet. |
| **Maximum elevation:** | 400 feet. |
| **Topographic Maps:** | Bonneville Dam USGS, Bonneville Dam Green Trial, Pacific Crest National Scenic Trail Washington Southern Section USFS. |

**Finding the Trailhead:** From Portland, take Interstate 84 to Cascade Locks and cross the Columbia River on the Bridge of the Gods, after paying a toll of 75 cents. Turn left, heading west on Washington State Highway 14, for 1.5 miles. The trailhead is on the right, to the north, opposite the Bonneville Visitor Center turnoff.

**Key points:**
0.5   Junction with PCT 2000
2.5   Gillette Lake

# GILLETTE LAKE AND TABLE MOUNTAIN

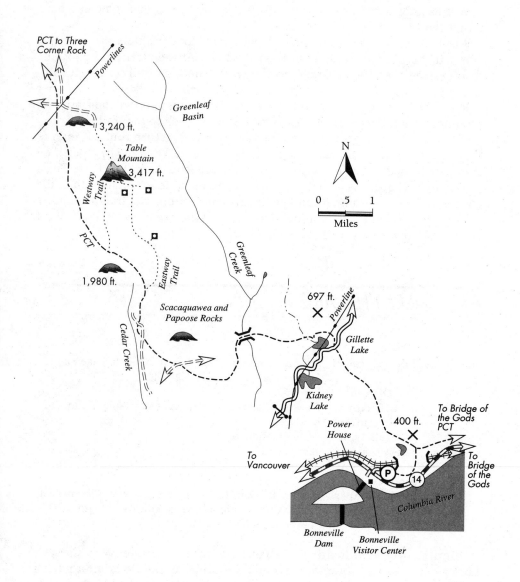

PCT to Three
Corner Rock

Powerlines

Greenleaf
Basin

3,240 ft.

Table
Mountain
3,417 ft.

Westway
Trail

PCT

1,980 ft.

Eastway
Trail

Cedar Creek

Scacaquawea and
Papoose Rocks

Greenleaf
Creek

N

0    .5    1
Miles

697 ft.

Powerline

Gillette
Lake

Kidney
Lake

400 ft.

To Bridge of
the Gods
PCT

To
Vancouver

Power
House

P

14

To
Bridge
of the
Gods

Columbia River

Bonneville
Dam

Bonneville
Visitor Center

**The trail:** This trail offers easy day-hiking. The terrain is dominated by second growth Douglas-fir trees averaging 60-80 years and younger. Most of the hiking is through the trees, but several points offer unique views of the Columbia River Gorge and Table Mountain.

The first 0.5 mile follows a singletrack path which crosses several jeep trails and offers views of the Columbia River. The strong current is visible here in the rippling and churning of the river. The trail actually runs on top of a train tunnel, and the passing by of a freight train might startle you. This section that connects with the PCT 2000 from the Bridge of the Gods is the Tamonous Trail, named after a Native American vision quest.

At 0.5 mile the Tamanous Trail intersects the PCT 2000. Turn left, heading north, to head for Gillette Lake. Several ponds to the west give the forest a smooth green tint. The trail winds around for a half a mile or so until reaching a Washington State Department of Natural Resources sign promoting sustainable yield and multiple-use timber harvest in the forest. The sign is an interesting cultural exhibit, considering how dissenters have altered the message with graffiti. After another 0.5 mile the trail passes through a clearcut from 1991 that was replanted a year later. The end of the clearcut affords a western view of the Gorge and the Beacon Rock Hike.

Just before reaching Gillette Lake, the trail crosses a forest road and continues underneath the powerlines. The trail drops a little, traverses the northeast slope above Gillette Lake, and then descends further to the lake's elevation. Despite the proximity of the road and powerlines, Gillette Lake is very quaint and natural. It is common to see waterfowl swimming in the calm water.

At an old tractor tire, a path forks off to the left, heading south, and leads down to a well-used campsite by the shore. The right fork, heading northwest, continues the PCT. Follow the same trail back to the trailhead and don't forget to turn west, back onto the Tamanous Trail.

See Map on Page 148

| | |
|---|---|
| **General description:** | A tough, 15-mile round-trip climb to the top of Table Mountain on the Pacific Crest Trail (PCT). |
| **Distance:** | 15.4 miles. |
| **Difficulty:** | Difficult. |
| **Traffic:** | Moderate to light. |
| **Trail type:** | Well-maintained to the Eastway junction, primitive to the summit. |
| **Best season:** | Year-round |
| **Elevation gain:** | 3,297 feet. |
| **Maximum elevation:** | 3,417 feet. |
| **Topographic maps:** | Bonneville Dam USGS, Bonneville Dam Green Trial, Pacific Crest National Scenic Trail Washington Southern Section USFS. |

**Finding the trailhead:** From Portland, take Interstate 84 to Cascade Locks and cross the Columbia River on the Bridge of the Gods after paying a toll of 75 cents. Turn left and head west on Washington State Highway 14 for 1.5 miles. The trailhead is on the right, opposite the Bonneville Visitor Center turnoff.

*Hikers on Dog Mountain Trail.*

**Key points:**
- 0.5   Junction with PCT 2000
- 2.5   Gillette Lake
- 4.0   Overlook
- 7.7   Table Mountain

**Note:** This trail is built and maintained by the Mazama Trail Club and is not an officially designated USFS trail.

**The trail:** This trail is one of the better Gorge power climbs. The terrain is dominated by second-growth Douglas-fir trees. Most of the hiking is through the trees, but the summit of Table Mountain is one of the more satisfying and spectacular destinations in the Gorge.

The first 0.5 mile follows a singletrack path which crosses several jeep trails and offers some views of the Columbia River. The trail is actually right on top of a train tunnel and the passing of a freight train might startle you. The section that connects with the PCT from the Bridge of the Gods is called the Tamonous Trail.

At 0.5 miles the Tamanous Trail intersects the PCT 2000. Turn left, heading north, to head for Gillette Lake. Several ponds to the west give a smooth green tint to the forest. After another 0.5 mile the trail passes through a clearcut from 1991. The end of the clearcut affords a western view of the Gorge and the Beacon Rock Hike.

*The top of Dog Mountain is a popular picnic area for the hardy hiker.*

Just before reaching Gillette Lake, the trail crosses a forest road and continues underneath the powerlines. The trail drops down to traverse the northeast slope above Gillette Lake, then drops farther to the lake's elevation. Despite the proximity of the road and powerlines, Gillette Lake is very quaint and natural-seeming. It is common to see waterfowl swimming in the calm water.

At an old tractor tire, a spur trail forks off to the left, heading south. It leads down to a well-used campsite by the shore. Camping is allowed, but expect to see a few dayhikers.

The main trail to the right, heading northwest, continues on to the PCT. Soon after leaving the lake the trail crosses Gillette Creek on a log bridge. No fording is necessary.

The trail climbs gradually until it crosses a jeep road; follow the singletrack trail with  Pacific Crest Trail markers northwest. Then pass a small pond to the west, just before Greenleaf Creek. A well-maintained footbridge across the creek affords views of Table Mountain. This is also a good place to filter some water.

After Greenleaf Creek the trail proceeds up steeper switchbacks for 0.25 mile to a break in the trees. This overlook offers views of Kidney Lake and across the Gorge to Wauna Point.

After the lookout is another unmarked junction; continue straight to a four-way junction and keep going straight. As Cedar Creek comes into view on the left and Papoose Rock becomes visible through the trees on the right, the trail crosses another jeep road. Stay straight again, heading north. Just 0.3 mile later, recross the jeep road and head up and right to the north. The left trail leads to a campsite where water is available.

Soon after the trail reaches the Eastway Trail. It is 1 mile to the summit of Table Mountain from this junction. Turn right, heading north, for a steep climb to the top. If you prefer a slightly less steep, but far from easy trail, continue northwest to the Westway.

The Eastway Trail is a heartbreaker trail, as indicated by the warning symbol at the bottom of the trail sign. The trail climbs through young forest, with views across the Gorge. You may think you're close to the top, but you're wrong; there is a false summit that makes for a good rest stop, with a view of steep basalt cliffs and the Cascades to the north. There are plenty of huckleberry bushes as you get higher. The path ducks through the bushes and scales some rocky places, but eventually the trail breaks out onto a grassy slope for the final march to the top. I did this last section in the fog and my friends kept asking me what it looked like ahead, but I couldn't see any more than they could: a steep grassy slope with a rutted trail. The top of Table Mountain is just as spectacular as it looks from the interstate and you can see a hell of a lot more. . . if it isn't foggy.

When you reach the summit, the trail forks to the right, and heads east to a nice clifftop lunch spot. The trail to the left, heading west, leads to shelter in the trees and the Westway Trail. You can follow the trail along the cliffs or through the trees. If you go through the trees, then as the trail forks head right, to the west, to follow the ridge to the PCT. The left trail, to the south, heads down on the Westway Trail. It is steep, but a little easier on your knees than the Eastway. When you reach the bottom, turn left on the PCT and head for home.

## 46 DOG MOUNTAIN LOOP

| | |
|---|---|
| **General description:** | A steep day hike up Dog Mountain. |
| **Distance:** | 6.8 miles. |
| **Difficulty:** | Difficult. |
| **Traffic:** | Heavy, but the trail can absorb a lot of use without feeling crowded. |
| **Trail type:** | Well-maintained. |
| **Best season:** | Year-round, depending on frost line. |
| **Elevation gain:** | 2,828 feet. |
| **Maximum elevation:** | 2,948 feet. |
| **Topographic maps:** | Mount Defiance USGS and Hood River Green Trails. |

**Finding the Trailhead:** From Portland, take Interstate 84 east to exit 44 at Cascade Locks. Cross the Bridge of the Gods after paying a toll of 75 cents. Turn right, heading east on Washington State Highway 14 for 12.5 miles to the well-marked Dog Mountain Trailhead on the left. Bathrooms are available 100 yards up from the old Dog Mountain Trailhead that is at the east end of the parking lot. The newer Augspurger Mountain Trailhead is just 50 feet west.

### Key points:
- 0.1 Public restrooms
- 0.5 Junction with Scenic and Old Route
- 2.0 Junction with return of Scenic and Old Route
- 2.5 Flowering Interno
- 2.8 Junction with loop trail
- 3.0 Junction with the Augspurger Trail
- 3.1 Summit
- 3.2 Return to Augspurger Trail
- 4.0 Junction with the Augspurger Trail
- 6.8 Return to trailhead

**The trail:** The Dog Mountain Trail System is heavily used by many hikers and the summit is often crowded on weekends; still, the mountain provides a peaceful and scenic hike. On a clear day, Mount Hood, Mount St. Helens, and Mount Adams are all visible from the top. Dog Mountain is also well-known for wildflowers, especially during the spring and early summer.

There are several different routes up Dog Mountain. The most scenic starts at the old trailhead at the east end of the parking lot. Take the "Scenic" option on the first loop and return either the same way or via the more gradual route down the backside. This description follows that route. You could reverse this by taking the Augspurger Trail up, which takes 3.7 miles to get to the top and is not as steep. I believe it makes a better route down, because a steep climb followed by a more gradual descent is easier on the knees.

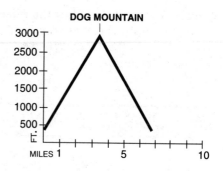

# DOG MOUNTAIN LOOP

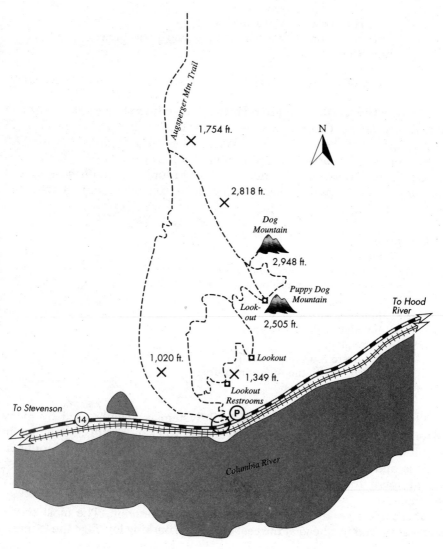

From the east end of the parking lot the trail climbs less than 0.1 mile to the public restrooms. Because of the trail's heavy use, it is better to use these now than to have to go along the trail somewhere. It continues to climb steeply up dry, partially exposed switchbacks through fir and oak trees. The trail reaches the first junction at 0.5 mile. The right trail, to the east, is the more gradual and scenic option. The left trail, to the northeast, is the oldest route up Dog Mountain and has no views, lots of shade, and steep grades.

After taking the right trail, climb past a couple of good viewpoints of the Columbia River and across to Mount Defiance. At 2 miles the scenic and old trails rejoin. (A shorter option is to turn back at this point, descending on the opposite loop trail.) The main trail climbs in the shade for another 0.5 mile until it opens up to the Flowering Interno. You might suppose this is a misprint or a bad pun on the "Towering Inferno," but that is what the junction sign says. As the trail opens up into a meadow, the blooms of paintbrush and balsamroot are spectacular. Even before these more noticeable flowers bloom, goldstars and buttercups add a yellow tint to the fresh green grass.

At 2.5 miles is a junction with a loop. This viewpoint junction is actually Puppy Dog Mountain, just a little bit smaller than the real thing. It used to be where the fire lookout was and it is easy to see why from the view. The left route, to the northwest, is more scenic, especially if the balsamroot are in full bloom. It stays in the open, allowing a full view of the flowers, river, and the mountains beyond. The right trail to the east is a slightly longer option with fewer views.

After turning left, traverse the west face of Dog Mountain to the intersection with the summit trail. Continuing straight north is the Augspurger Trail; turning right, a little to the east, takes you to the top and the loop trail to the "Puppy Dog" junction. Turn right to reach the top. Just before the summit, the trail keeps going straight and passes a short spur trail on the left, to the north, through some low brush. This path is necessary to actually reach the highest point, but the view is better just below. The meadow below is a comfortable lunch and water spot.

 On steep climbs, drinking lots of water helps prevent the ill effects of dehydration and exhaustion. These are two major contributors to hypothermia, on both warm and cool days alike.

From inside the grove of trees at the summit you can see Mount Adams (and, through the branches, Mount St. Helens) to the north. Mount Hood and Mount Defiance are easily seen to the south across the river.

To return to the trailhead there are three options: 1) the way you came; 2) the return trail to Puppy Dog Junction; and 3) the gentle, longer route back down the Augspurger Trail. For the last option, turn right down the 0.1 mile trail to the to the junction with the Augspurger Trail. Turn right again, heading northwest, for the additional the 3.7 miles back to the trailhead.

The trail to the Augsperger Trail along the west face of Dog Mountain descends gradually, entering the trees after 0.5 mile. At 1 mile from the top it intersects with the Augspurger Mountain Trail, scheduled to reopen as a primitive hiking trail in 1997. Turn left for the trailhead, just 2.8 miles farther. The trail descends gradually along the side of Dog Mountain back toward the Gorge, down a couple of switchbacks and some dry, exposed scree slopes. Watch for poison oak.

## 47   CATHERINE CREEK NATURAL ARCH

| | |
|---|---|
| **General description:** | A short day hike to a natural basalt arch. |
| **Distance:** | 1.4 miles. |
| **Difficulty:** | Easy. |
| **Traffic:** | Moderate. |
| **Trail type:** | Jeep trail. |
| **Best season:** | Year-round. |
| **Elevation gain:** | 360 ft. |
| **Maximum elevation:** | 600 ft. |
| **Topographic maps:** | Lyle Wash, USGS. |

**Finding the trailhead:** From Portland, take Interstate 84 east to Hood River. Take the Hood River exit, cross the $1 toll bridge, and turn right, heading east, on Washington State Highway 14 for 6 miles. Then turn left, heading north, on old Highway 14 for 1.5 miles. A Forest Service gate is on the left before the washed-out bridge over Catherine Creek

**Key points:**
    0.3   Jeep road forks
    0.4   Jeep road forks

*SPECIAL REGULATIONS FOR CATHERINE CREEK AREA*
    1. No fires.
    2. No motorized vehicles.
    3. All other modes of travel are legal.

**The trail:** There is a controversy in this area over what types of use are permitted. Motorized vehicles are not allowed currently, but the Forest Service is studying the issue. If there is a trailhead questionnaire, filling it out and relaying that you used this area for hiking might help determine future management.

At the trailhead there are two jeep roads; take the one on your right, heading northeast, dropping into the Catherine Creek Gulch. Catherine Creek will most likely not have much water, if any, but it does have plenty of poison oak.

# CATHERINE CREEK NATURAL ARCH

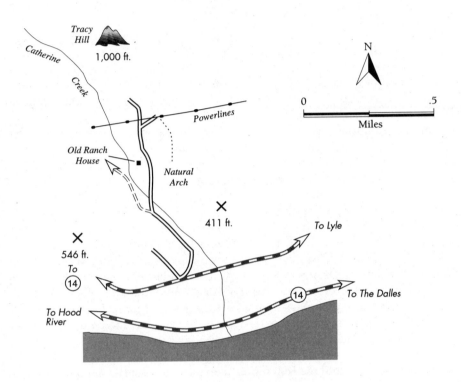

At 0.3 mile stay right, heading northeast, at the fork. The road soon passes an old corral to the west. Look up to the east, on the right, to see the natural arch. If the old ranch and this view of the arch are enough entertainment, return via the same route. If you would like a better view from atop the arch, continue up the jeep road to the north. The forest consists of Oregon oak, ponderosa pine, and some poison oak.

After a climb the road divides again; stay right, heading east. Just a little farther, under the powerlines, is a faint path veering right, to the south. A cross-country route leads across the brown grass atop the basalt to a lookout above the arch.

The view of the arch is a bit eerie, as a narrow slit allows light to slip between the arch and the side of the gulch. You might be tempted to scramble down underneath the arch to the gulch, but this route involves some tricky tallus slope sliding on large, loose pieces of basalt. Basalt makes for a very coarse surface against your skin if you fall.

It is better to return via the original route.

# APPENDIX A: HAPPY HIKING AND HEAVY USE

We all want our own wilderness area all to ourselves, but that only happens in our dreams. Lots of people use the Gorge, and to make everyone's experience better, we all must work at politely sharing the wilderness.

For example, hikers must share trails with backcountry horsemen and mountain bikers. Both groups have every right to be on approved trails, so please do not turn an encounter into a confrontation.

Another example of politely sharing the wilderness is choosing your campsite. If you get to a popular lake late in the day and all the good campsites are taken, don't crowd in on another camper. This is most aggravating, as these sites rightfully go on a first-come, first-served basis. If you're late, it's your responsibility to move on or to take a less desirable site at a respectful distance away from other campers.

Also, special considerations are warranted for very popular trails like Multnomah Falls and Eagle Creek. Going to Multnomah Falls on a busy summer weekend is a different experience for the veteran hiker. It is crowded. The trail is paved. Orange fences section off rehabilitation areas. Signs at every switchback promise fines for cutting. People in high heels with radios and dressed for a city park tromp up the path. Increasingly, areas like Multnomah Falls that receive extremely heavy use have to be managed like city parks, and other areas may have a similar future.

I have hiked up to the falls many times and would not hesitate to do it again. People have told me that other hikers are necessarily a negative when choosing a hike. Yet people will always keep coming to Multnomah Falls. More diverse groups of hikers get a first-hand look at nature here than anywhere else in the Gorge. Everyone has the right to care for the preservation of Multnomah Falls. The more wilderness advocates the better.

Even so, places like Multnomah Falls require extra patience and energy. I recommend these guidelines for happy hiking with heavy use:

1. A simple, friendly howdy or hello is worth a thousand nods or shrugs.
2. Yield generously to other hikers, especially tiny ones.
3. Don't bring noisemakers.
4. Avoid excessive public displays of affection.
5. Support the volunteers and public workers that have the difficult job of managing this treasure.

# APPENDIX B: HIKER'S CHECKLIST

## CLOTHING

In general, strive for natural fibers such as cotton and wool, and choose earth tones instead of neon colors. Your wilderness partners will appreciate it. This might not apply in hunting season when a bright color such as safety orange is preferred. Try out the clothing before leaving home. In particular, make sure your boots are broken in, lest they break you on the first day of the hike. Get good raingear. Weather in the Gorge is often wet. You absolutely need high-quality raingear.

Pack enough clothes to keep you warrm—regardless of how hot it is when you leave the trailhead or if your pack already seems too heavy. Leave something else at home instead of warm clothes.

**Day Hiking Clothes:**

- ❑ Stocking cap
- ❑ Wool gloves
- ❑ Raingear (pants and coat 100% waterproof)
- ❑ Long underwear (preferably synthetic)
- ❑ Sweater
- ❑ Hiking shorts
- ❑ One pair your favorite socks and one pair wool socks
- ❑ Large-brimmed hat or cap
- ❑ Lightweight hiking boots
- ❑ T-shirt

**Additional Clothes for Overnight Trips or Extreme Weather Conditions:**

- ❑ Water-resistant, windproof wilderness coat
- ❑ Lightweight, long-sleeve shirts or T-shirts
- ❑ Short-sleeve shirts or T-shirts
- ❑ Sandals or lightweight shoes for fording streams and wearing in camp
- ❑ One pair of socks for each day, plus one extra pair of light hiking socks and one extra pair of heavy wool socks
- ❑ Extra fleece or sweater
- ❑ One pair wool pants or sweat pants

## HIKING EQUIPMENT

Equipment does not have to be new or fancy (or expensive), but make sure you test everything before you leave home.

### Day Hiking Equipment:

- ❏ Day pack or fanny pack
- ❏ Water bottles (full)
- ❏ Compass
- ❏ Maps
- ❏ Toilet trowel
- ❏ Toilet paper
- ❏ Sunblock
- ❏ Flashlight and extra batteries
- ❏ Pocket knife and tweezers
- ❏ Sunglasses
- ❏ Survival kit
- ❏ First-aid kit
- ❏ Water filter or water purification tablets

### Additional Equipment for Overnight Trips in Gorge:

- ❏ Tent and waterproof fly
- ❏ Sleeping bag (20 degrees F. or warmer) and stuff sack
- ❏ Sleeping pad
- ❏ Cooking pots and pot holder
- ❏ Wire screen for sifting dishwater
- ❏ Full-size backpack
- ❏ Cup, bowl, and eating utensils
- ❏ Lightweight camp stove and adequate fuel
- ❏ Garbage bags
- ❏ Zip lock bags
- ❏ Nylon cord (50 feet)
- ❏ Tarp (lightweight nylon)
- ❏ Small towel
- ❏ Personal items (toothbrush and paste)

## FOOD

For day hiking, bring fruit and high-energy bars or sandwiches for lunch. For overnight trips bring enough food, including lots of high-energy snacks for lunching during the day. Plan meals carefully, bringing just enough food, plus some emergency rations. Avoid fresh, smelly foods and canned foods. Freeze-dried foods are the lightest and safest, but expensive and not really necessary. Don't forget hot and cold drinks.

# MISCELLANEOUS

- ☐ Paper towels
- ☐ Binoculars
- ☐ Camera and extra film
- ☐ Fishing equipment and permits
- ☐ Insect repellent
- ☐ Your FalconGuide

# ABOUT THE AUTHOR

Russ Schneider grew up hiking the wilds of the West. He moved to Portland to attend Reed College. While earning a degree in Portland, Russ visited the Gorge often for a taste of the wilderness. Its accessibility from the city and its truly wild character kept Russ hiking, and pretty soon he had hiked every one of the trails in this book.

As a veteran hiker and guide with Glacier Wilderness Guides, Russ loves showing people the land. Russ revised *Hiking Montana* to start his writing career. In addition to *Hiking the Columbia River Gorge*, he is currently working on *Fishing Glacier, Backpacking Tips*, and a revision of *Fishing Montana*, while developing a new series of outdoor books for Falcon.

**FALCON** GUIDES ® are available for where-to-go hiking, mountain biking, rock climbing, walking, scenic driving, fishing, rockhounding, paddling, birding, wildlife viewing, and camping. We also have FalconGuides on essential outdoor skills and subjects and field identification. The following titles are currently available, but this list grows every year. For a free catalog with a complete list of titles, call FALCON toll-free at 1-800-582-2665.

### HIKING GUIDES

Hiking Alaska
Hiking Alberta
Hiking Arizona
Hiking Arizona's Cactus Country
Hiking the Beartooths
Hiking Big Bend National Park
Hiking Bob Marshall Country
Hiking California
Hiking California's Desert Parks
Hiking Carlsbad Caverns
   and Guadalupe Mtns. National Parks
Hiking Colorado
Hiking the Columbia River Gorge
Hiking Florida
Hiking Georgia
Hiking Glacier & Waterton Lakes National Parks
Hiking Grand Canyon National Park
Hiking Grand Staircase-Escalante/Glen Canyon
Hiking Great Basin National Park
Hiking Hot Springs in the Pacific Northwest
Hiking Idaho
Hiking Maine
Hiking Michigan
Hiking Minnesota
Hiking Montana
Hiker's Guide to Nevada
Hiking New Hampshire
Hiking New Mexico

Hiking New York
Hiking North Cascades
Hiking Northern Arizona
Hiking Olympic National Park
Hiking Oregon
Hiking Oregon's Eagle Cap Wilderness
Hiking Oregon's Mount Hood/Eagle Cap
Hiking Oregon's Three Sisters Country
Hiking Pennsylvania
Hiking Shenandoah National Park
Hiking South Carolina
Hiking South Dakota's Black Hills Country
Hiking Southern New England
Hiking Tennessee
Hiking Texas
Hiking Utah
Hiking Utah's Summits
Hiking Vermont
Hiking Virginia
Hiking Washington
Hiking Wisconsin
Hiking Wyoming
Hiking Wyoming's Wind River Range
Hiking Yellowstone National Park
Hiking Zion & Bryce Canyon National Parks
The Trail Guide to Bob Marshall Country
Wild Montana
Wild Utah

get
**FALCON** GUIDED

---

## Scenic Driving Guides

Scenic Driving Alaska and the Yukon
Scenic Driving Arizona
Scenic Driving the Beartooth Highway
Scenic Driving California
Scenic Driving Colorado
Scenic Driving Florida
Scenic Driving Georgia
Scenic Driving Hawaii
Scenic Driving Idaho
Scenic Driving Michigan
Scenic Driving Minnesota
Scenic Driving Montana
Scenic Driving New England
Scenic Driving New Mexico
Scenic Driving North Carolina
Scenic Driving Oregon
Scenic Driving the Ozarks including the
   Ouchita Mountains
Scenic Driving Texas
Scenic Driving Utah
Scenic Driving Washington
Scenic Driving Wisconsin
Scenic Driving Wyoming
Back Country Byways
National Forest Scenic Byways
National Forest Scenic Byways II

## Historic Trail Guides

Traveling California's Gold Rush Country
Traveling the Lewis & Clark Trail
Traveling the Oregon Trail
Traveler's Guide to the Pony Express Trail

## Wildlife Viewing Guides

Alaska Wildlife Viewing Guide
Arizona Wildlife Viewing Guide
California Wildlife Viewing Guide
Colorado Wildlife Viewing Guide
Florida Wildlife Viewing Guide
Idaho Wildlife Viewing Guide
Indiana Wildlife Vewing Guide
Iowa Wildlife Viewing Guide
Kentucky Wildlife Viewing Guide
Massachusetts Wildlife Viewing Guide
Montana Wildlife Viewing Guide
Nebraska Wildlife Viewing Guide
Nevada Wildlife Viewing Guide
New Hampshire Wildlife Viewing Guide
New Jersey Wildlife Viewing Guide
New Mexico Wildlife Viewing Guide
New York Wildlife Viewing Guide
North Carolina Wildlife Viewing Guide
North Dakota Wildlife Viewing Guide
Ohio Wildlife Viewing Guide
Oregon Wildlife Viewing Guide
Tennessee Wildlife Viewing Guide
Texas Wildlife Viewing Guide
Utah Wildlife Viewing Guide
Vermont Wildlife Viewing Guide
Virginia Wildlife Viewing Guide
Washington Wildlife Viewing Guide
West Virginia Wildlife Viewing Guide
Wisconsin Wildlife Viewing Guide

---

■ *To order any of these books, check with your local bookseller*
*or call FALCON® at **1-800-582-2665**.*

*Visit us on the world wide web at:*
www.falconguide.com

FALCON®

get
**FALCON**GUIDED

## BEST EASY DAY HIKES SERIES

Beartooths
Canyonlands & Arches
Best Hikes on the Continental Divide
Glacier & Wateron Lakes
Grand Staircase-Escalante and the Glen Canyon
    Region
Grand Canyon
North Cascades
Olympics
Shenandoah
Yellowstone

## 12 SHORT HIKES SERIES

### Colorado

Aspen
Boulder
Denver Foothills Central
Denver Foothills North
Denver Foothills South
Rocky Mountain National Park-Estes Park
Rocky Mountain National Park-Grand Lake
Steamboat Springs
Summit County
Vail

### California

San Diego Coast
San Diego Mountains
San Francisco Bay Area-Coastal
San Francisco Bay Area-East Bay
San Francisco Bay Area-North Bay
San Francisco Bay Area-South Bay

### Washington

Mount Rainier National Park-Paradise
Mount Rainier National Park-Sunrise

FALCON®

■ *To order any of these books, check with your local bookseller*
*or call FALCON® at **1-800-582-2665**.*

*Visit us on the world wide web at:*
www.falconguide.com

**get FALCON GUIDED**

**FALCON GUIDES** ® are available for where-to-go hiking, mountain biking, rock climbing, walking, scenic driving, fishing, rockhounding, paddling, birding, wildlife viewing, and camping. We also have FalconGuides on essential outdoor skills and subjects and field identification. The following titles are currently available, but this list grows every year. For a free catalog with a complete list of titles, call FALCON toll-free at 1-800-582-2665.

## HIKING GUIDES:

**State-specific guides** to Alaska, Alberta, Arizona, California, Colorado, Florida, Georgia, Idaho, Maine, Michigan, Minnesota, Montana, Nevada, New Hampshire, New Mexico, New York, North Carolina, Oregon, Pennsylvania, South Carolina, Tennessee, Texas, Utah, Vermont, Virginia, Washington, and Wyoming.

**Regional guides** to Arizona's Cactus Country, the Beartooths, Big Bend, Bob Marshall Country, California's Desert Parks, Canyonlands & Arches, Carlsbad Caverns & Guadalupe Mnts., Columbia River Gorge, Glacier & Waterton Lakes, Grand Canyon, Grand Staircase-Escalante/Glen Canyon, Great Basin, Hot Springs of the Pacific Northwest, North Cascades, Northern Arizona, Olympic Nat. Park, Oregon's Eagle Cap Wilderness, Oregon's Mount Hood/Badger Creek, Oregon's Three Sister's Country, Shenandoah, South Dakota's Black Hills Country, Southern New England, Utah's Summits, Wyoming's Wind River Range, Yellowstone, and Zion & Bryce Canyon.

**Best Easy Day Hikes** to the Beartooths, Canyonlands & Arches, on the Continental Divide, Glacier & Waterton Lakes, Glen Canyon, Grand Canyon, North Cascades, and Yellowstone

## MOUNTAIN BIKING GUIDES:

Arizona, Colorado, Georgia, New Mexico, New York, Northern New England, Oregon, South Carolina, Southern New England, Utah, and Wisconsin.

Local mountain biking guides to Bend, Boise, Bozeman, Chequamegon, Colorado Springs Denver-Boulder, Durango, Helena, Moab, and White Mountains (West).

## WILDLIFE VIEWING GUIDES:

Alaska, Arizona, California, Colorado, Florida, Idaho, Indiana, Iowa, Kentucky, Massachusetts, Montana, Nebraska, Nevada, New Hampshire, New Jersey, New Mexico, New York, North Carolina, North Dakota, Ohio, Oregon, Tennessee, Texas, Utah, Vermont, Virginia, Washington, West Virginia, and Wisconsin

## SCENIC DRIVING:

Alaska/Yukon, Arizona, Beartooth Highway, California, Colorado, Florida, Georgia, Hawaii, Idaho, Michigan, Minnesota, Montana, New England, New Mexico, North Carolina, Oregon, Ozarks, Texas, Utah, Washington, Wisconsin and Wyoming. Plus, Back Country Byways, National Forest Scenic Byways, and National Forest Scenic Byways II. Historic trail driving guides to California's Gold Rush Country, Lewis and Clark Trail, the Pony Express Trail, and the Oregon Trail.

■ *To order any of these books, check with your local bookseller or call FALCON® at 1-800-582-2665.*
*Visit us on the world wide web at:*
www.falconguide.com

FALCON®